Erick Valdes

# Bioethical Principlism

## Origins, Foundations and Problems

VDM Verlag Dr. Müller

**Impressum/Imprint (nur für Deutschland/ only for Germany)**
Bibliografische Information der Deutschen Nationalbibliothek: Die Deutsche Nationalbibliothek verzeichnet diese Publikation in der Deutschen Nationalbibliografie; detaillierte bibliografische Daten sind im Internet über http://dnb.d-nb.de abrufbar.


Coverbild: www.ingimage.com

Verlag: VDM Verlag Dr. Müller GmbH & Co. KG
Dudweiler Landstr. 99, 66123 Saarbrücken, Deutschland
Telefon +49 681 9100-698, Telefax +49 681 9100-988
Email: info@vdm-verlag.de

Herstellung in Deutschland:
Schaltungsdienst Lange o.H.G., Berlin
Books on Demand GmbH, Norderstedt
Reha GmbH, Saarbrücken
Amazon Distribution GmbH, Leipzig
**ISBN: 978-3-639-37162-8**

**Imprint (only for USA, GB)**
Bibliographic information published by the Deutsche Nationalbibliothek: The Deutsche Nationalbibliothek lists this publication in the Deutsche Nationalbibliografie; detailed bibliographic data are available in the Internet at http://dnb.d-nb.de.


Cover image: www.ingimage.com

Publisher: VDM Verlag Dr. Müller GmbH & Co. KG
Dudweiler Landstr. 99, 66123 Saarbrücken, Germany
Phone +49 681 9100-698, Fax +49 681 9100-988
Email: info@vdm-publishing.com

Printed in the U.S.A.
Printed in the U.K. by (see last page)
**ISBN: 978-3-639-37162-8**

To Marlenne

# CONTENTS

# ACKNOWLEDGMENTS

This book has benefited from a relevant array of critical and helpful comments by scholars both from the Center for Clinical Bioethics and the Kennedy Institute of Ethics at Georgetown University. Without their significant contribution every chapter would have been diminished.

My arguments in chapter I. were influenced by Hans-Martin Sass who provided me important theoretical references on Fritz Jahr's work. His disinterested collaboration improved significantly the accuracy and depth of my perspective. I also owe a deep debt of gratitude to Ed Pellegrino, Carol Taylor and Bob Barnet for the improvement of chapters II. and III. Their constructive comments and precise suggestions greatly clarified my ideas.

I thank my research assistant at Georgetown University, Pablo Mahu, who searched and summarized several theoretical sources by facilitating my work in some parts of this book.

Also, I want to thank my beloved wife Marlenne who is the inspiration of all my efforts and initiatives. I am totally grateful for her unconditional support and lovely presence.

Finally, I thank the National Fund for Scientific and Technological Development (Fondo Nacional de Desarrollo Cientifico y Tecnologico, FONDECYT) of the Government of Chile, which through the post-doctoral scholarship assigned to my project 3100012 has made this book possible.

Washington, DC, May 2011

# INTRODUCTION

The techno-scientific development in the last sixty years has permitted significant progress but has also generated great dangers. This new capability indicates the particular scope of human technology. Nevertheless, during most of its history, mankind has existed with technology. Until now, its relationship to the world and nature has been one of mutual assistance, since previous technological development lacked the idea of progress that characterizes current human beings' existence.

Technology and its consequences have not only altered how humans interpret the world but have created the ability to artificially transform that experience. Scientists have an unusual power which allows performing what seemed impossible a few years earlier. Possibilities of creating life through genetic manipulation have produced an insatiable appetite for discovery but have also raised moral questions about what the limit of techno-scientific actions should be. Some emblematic cases of abuse in human beings through experimentation stressed the need to regulate the medical and scientific *praxis*.

It was thought that the type of reflection that should be conducted to find regulatory procedures in the fields of human experimentation and the physician-patient relationship should not be done only by physicians and scientists. The reflection on these matters corresponded, in fact, to the whole of society, represented by different actors from different fields of knowledge. In accordance with the above mentioned, The National Commission for the Protection of Human Subjects was established by the Congress of the United States in the early seventies, and later the Belmont Report was published.

The main objective of those initiatives was to regulate medical and scientific practices, not merely through common sense or interdisciplinary dialogue, but through the creation of principles under which all rational and reasonable individuals could share a universal morality.

Those principles became a kind of reference and guide for rational debate and deliberation in particularly complex cases, and thereby contributed to achieve solutions by directing the reasoning and dialogue among all involved in it. Those theoretical guidelines are based on our ethical and axiological tradition and have recovered the respect for inalienable rights and duties, which had been forgotten in the maelstrom of biotechnological empowerment and development.

While these principles undoubtedly are a huge breakthrough for bioethical deliberation around sensitive issues raised in the heart of science and medicine, they still encounter major difficulties in their application in the practical realm. This situation is originated in several different causes: deficiencies in the foundations of the principles, problems in the logic of their definitions, ignorance of their limits and scope, and diversity of interpretations about their meaning and real degree of applicability. Therefore, any principle means a theoretical conceptual framework of an abstract nature, and requires a hermeneutic approach; namely, it needs to be interpreted. This impedes the consensus about its application in practical fields.

As principles are a framework of general character and moral problems are always of a particular nature, the two can collide in practice, especially when they are applied to particularly conflicting and complex cases. Beyond the foundational works of Jahr, Potter and Hellegers, bioethics has needed to acquire more coherence and unity in its content and thereby to transform its principles into plausible criteria that satisfy all the necessary requirements to guide an effective deliberation and to reach an appropriate solution for complex moral problems, the likes of which Ethics has never had to face in the entire course of human history.

The first edition of Beauchamp and Childress' seminal book, *Principles of Biomedical Ethics* appeared in 1979. This work has been the most universally accepted statement of bioethical principles. Its authors consider important topics of Ross and Frankena's ethics for further definition of the principles, but it is also possible to find in their work important conceptual antecedents in the thinking of Aristotle, Hume, Kant and Mill, among others. The effort of Beauchamp and Childress to create a dialogue between the two most important branches of Western moral reasoning (teleology and deontology) has been an important contribution to the theoretical deepening of bioethics, as well as a laudable effort to strengthen the basis of bioethics, especially if we consider that both Beauchamp and Childress come from different philosophical heritages.

Principles of biomedical ethics received a general acceptance in academic, clinical and scientific circles. However, this proposal has not been exempt from criticism, which has led the authors to make several modifications, redefinitions and extensions to the theoretical and methodological scope of the principles in subsequent editions. The criticisms are based mainly on what I have called "the problem of principlism," which could briefly be defined as the absence of one or more criteria for ranking the principles. Namely, the equivalence or theoretical equality of the principles constitute a problem when they are applied, since we do not have some convincing criterion that indicates which principle must be imposed on another and why.

For this reason some people think that bioethics is just a casuistic discipline that, ultimately, establishes a formal deliberative structure that can only be applied on some cases but that in most of them is unusable due to the contradiction between the principles in the practical realm. Notwithstanding the foregoing, Beauchamp and Childress's book has been an indisputable and undeniable contribution to the study of moral problems inherent to medical and scientific practice and it has also been an essential reference material to think about such problems and advancing towards their solution.

Beauchamp and Childress' attemp is an effort to systematize the approach to moral issues, to provide some rationality to bioethical deliberation, and to integrate argumentation and dialogue in moral reasoning. In this regard, the proposal of these authors tacitly understands bioethics as an intersubjective and dialogical discipline and argues that moral truth is not only in the individual consciousness but in the public space; that is, in the agreement generated by the argumentative and rational encounter of many subjects willing to seek and establish consensus about cross disciplinary issues that affect social harmony.

However, despite the efforts of Beauchamp and Childress, principles of biomedical ethics have certain formal defects that require the reformulation and extension of their content and meaning. Also, their proposal implies certain paraconsistency since faced with an insurmountable clash of principles we should use the casuistry as a criterion for determining their applicability. In short, this would mean to go back to opinions and personal judgments by narrowing the procedure's scope to the realm of subjectivity.

The question of whether or not the scope and degree of possibility of bioethical principlism refers to its relationship with the current moral scenario. Indeed, an analysis of the status of bioethical principlism should be linked, obligatorily, with the contemporary moral situation, in which science and technology have reached such a degree of development that they have relegated moral philosophy to a second order, by reducing it to a subjective level of epistemic-ontological irrationality and incompetence that diminishes the validity of its statements.

Bioethical principlism is a response to the contemporary interpellation of biotechnology and biomedicine, and it considers, as a fundamental task, the development of foundations and procedures to address new ethical conflicts in the context of intersubjective dialogue, based on a tacit recognition of a common humanity. In this dialogical and argumentative attitude, the ethics of responsibility of Jonas, discursive ethics of Habermas and Apel, analytic pluralism, and the ethics of moral strangers of Engelhardt attempting to design procedures that can guide moral bargainings. All these theoretical positions seek, in principle, to demolish the modern subject-object structure between man and world. There is consensus about this could mainly be achieved through an applied ethics, such as bioethics.

I have therefore considered the philosophical deepening of these procedural ethics as being fundamental, since the ideas that this area of thought can contribute towards the elucidation of its own moral problems of globalization have been shown to be relevant. However, the fact of answering the question about the real possibility of bioethical principlism has its main problem precisely in the way of founding the implementation of concrete procedures for the resolution of conflicts.

The encounter between traditional ethics and bioethics is undoubtedly problematic. Clarifying possible relationships between philosophical foundations of ethics and contents, problems and methods of bioethics, is not an easy task. It is common to think that bioethics is only the application of certain principles and rules in a specific field that has in theory moral rules and principles. In this sense: Is bioethics the same ethics as always, but confronted with new problems? Does the novelty lie within bioethics itself or among the issues that have been raised during the technological age? Does bioethics create a specific or unique type of knowledge? Is bioethics, conceived as an applied ethics, a strategic resource for asserting power and inducing moral consensuses that are shielded from public scrutiny?[1] Or, conversely, does it reflect a genuine attempt to permeate all human activities and practices with ethical content, as a way of reinforcing pluralistic societies?

Bioethics stems from a supposition, which is at the very least doubtful: an intuition of human nature, which leads to the discovery of elements that are shared by that nature, and that would facilitate a consensus among people with different values and beliefs. As it is only intuition, any attempt to universalize the acceptance of moral correctness criteria, from the concept of nature, is left truncated in bioethics. However, bioethics and its backbone "principlism" are plausible proposal to resolve and regulate moral issues that arise in the daily manifestation of human endeavor, whether they are public or private. This refers to a reasonable degree of applicability of the principles in the context of a pluralistic society, notwithstanding the constant tension between the grounds and procedures, which should be understood, not as a Hegelian dialectic, but as a complement that ought to be exploited, both in the methodological field as well as the epistemological one.

Consequently, bioethical principlism offers some interesting support to address moral problems, mainly because it has certain features that traditional ethics does not. First of all, bioethical principlism deals with specific problems that arise in professional and social practices, which substantially contribute to the creation of regulatory

---

[1] For a possible answer to this question, see: Macintyre, Alasdair, "Does Applied Ethics Rest on a Mistake?" in *The Monist*, 67, 1984, pp. 498-513.

pathways in line with the changes that have occurred as a result of technology and globalization. Secondly, it represents an effort to go beyond the typical divisions of a particular discipline. And thirdly, it proposes a dialogic communicative format that seems to be a direction that could be considered by all ethics that aspire to be in tune with the current conditions of existence.

In light of what I have already exposed, my task here will be to review and rethink the Beauchamp and Childress' bioethical principles by describing the problem of principlism and demonstrating why the epistemological and methodological aspects of it are still insufficient to address cases with a real degree of objectivity and impartiality. Finally, I will present a tentative formula that intends to overcome the contradiction between Beauchamp and Childress' principles in order to avoid paralyzing reasoning, deliberation and decision making in particularly complex scenarios.

However, before doing the above mentioned, I will return to the path of the founders of bioethics by reviewing the main milestones that influenced the emergence of the discipline and the need for theoretical guidelines and deliberative procedures to face the new moral problems arisen in the medical and scientific fields.

# I. ORIGINS

## I.1. Fritz Jahr and his Bio-Ethical Imperative

The main goal of this section is to demonstrate that Fritz Jahr should be considered the real father of bioethics since, in his absolutely pioneering work, is not only present the word – or the "sound" – bioethics, but also, and very especially, the first big lines of a brand new discipline.

Indeed, the concept "bioethics" was not born either in 1970 with the Van Rensselaer Potter's paper "Bioethics: The Science of Survival," or in 1971 with the establishment of the Kennedy Institute of Ethics at Georgetown University by Andre Hellegers, as many people think.[2] Fritz Jahr, a German protestant pastor, philosopher and educator published, in 1927, an editorial entitled "Bio-Ethik. Eine Umschau über die ethischen Beziehungen des Menschen zu Tier und Pflanze," ("Bio-Ethics. Reviewing the Ethical Relations of Humans towards Animals and Plants") in a leading German natural science

[2] Potter, Van Rensselaer "Bioethics: The Science of Survival," Persp. Biol. Med. 1970, 14(1): 127-153. For learning similarities and differences between Potter, Hellegers and Jahr's concepts, see Sass, Hans-Martin, "Fritz Jahr's 1927 Concept of Bioethics," *Kennedy Institute of Ethics Journal*, 2007, 17(4): 282.

journal called *Kosmos*, which prestige, as Hans-Martin Sass has said, is only comparable to current *Nature* and *Science.*[3] Thus, the origin of the concept bioethics must be placed 43 years before Potter published his famous work. In fact, we may consider the Potter's ideas about bioethics as a continuation of Jahr's seminal contribution even though Potter never quoted Jahr's writings either in his papers or books and Jahr's concept of bioethics is wider than Potter's since Jahr extends his concern towards all living beings.[4] It is not clear if Potter ever knew about Jahr or simply neglected him. The fact is that Potter has unfairly been considered as the pioneer of bioethics while the man who actually introduced the idea and also coined the term *bioethics* into philosophical and scientific fields has been forgotten.[5]

Fritz Jahr's work cannot only be reduced to the short writing that I have mentioned already. He also published an overwhelming array of papers on bioethics and other related topics between 1927 and 1938 which had no massive repercussions due to the German political circumstances of those days and the advent of World War II.[6] It is important to clarify here that the concept of bioethics that

---

[3] *Kosmos. Handweiser für Naturfreunde und Zentralblatt für das naturwissen-schaftliche Bildungs und Sammelwesen,* Stuttgart, 1927, 24(1): 2-4. Also see, Sass, Hans-Martin, "Poscriptum and References," in *Selected Essays in Bioethics 1927-1934 Fritz Jahr*, Zentrum für Medizinische Ethik, Bochum, November 2010, Issue 186, p. 24.

[4] When Potter published his paper he did not put a dash between "bio" and "ethics." Nevertheless, the meaning that underlies Potter's term is virtually the same as Jahr's.

[5] It is interesting to observe how the name of Fritz Jahr has not only been neglected by Potter but also by the most of bioethicists.

[6] *Bio-Ethik. 1927 (Bio-Ethics); Der Tod und die Tiere. 1928; Tierschutz und Ethik. 1928 (Animal Protection and Ethics); Soziale und sexuelle Ethik in der Tageszeitung. 1928 (Social and Sexual Ethics in the Daily Press); Wege zum sexuellen Ethos. 1928; Zwei ethische Probleme in ihrem Gegensatz und in ihrer Vereinigung im sozialen Leben. 1928;*

Jahr conceived was yet far from how we currently understand it, especially from a procedural point of view. Nevertheless, since his relevant approaches to humans-animals-nature relationships, social and sexual ethics, basic moral problems of social life, freedom of thought, education, moral law, the duty of self-preservation, and very especially because of his Bio-Ethical Imperative (*bio-ethische Imperativ*), Jahr deserves to be considered as the "Father of Bioethics," even though the name "bioethics" should still go through many paths in order to become the discipline we know today. I will try to pay the debt we owe Jahr by showing how valid his ideas still are and stressing his main contributions to the current bioethics.
In 1927 Jahr wrote:

> From Bio-Psychik it is only a step to Bio-Ethics, i.e. the assumption of moral obligations not only towards humans, but towards all forms of life. In reality, bio-ethics is not just a discovery of modern times. An especially attractive example from the past is the figure

---

*Egoism and Altruism. 1929; Gesinnungsdiktatur oder Gedankenfreiheit? 1930 (Character Dictate or Freedom of Thought); Unsere Zweifel an Gott. 1933; Drei Studiem zum 5. Gebot. 1934 (Three Studies on the Fifht Commandment); Jenseitsglaube und Ethik im Christentum. 1934; Die sittlich-soziale Bedeutung des Sonntags. 1934; Zweifel an Jesus? 1934; Ethische Betrachtungen zu innerkirchlichen Glaubenskämpfen. 1935; Glauben und Werkein ihrem Gegensatz und in ihrer Vereinigung. 1935; Drei Abschnitte des Lebens nach 2. Korinther. 1938.* I thank Dr. Hans-Martin Sass for having access to this comprehensive list of Jahr's writings as well as for sharing with me his precise and excellent analysis on Jahr's thought and his precise translations into English. (See, Sass, Hans-Martin, "Aufsäzte zur Bioethik 1927-1938 Fritz Jahr," Nachwort und Nachweise von Hans-Martin Sass, *Zentrum für Medizinische Ethik*, Bochum, Dezember, 2010; "Selected Essays in Bioethics 1927-1934 Fritz Jahr," *Zentrum für Medizinische Ethik*, Bochum, November 2010, Issue 186. Postcript and References by Hans-Martin Sass); and also, "Fritz Jahr's 1927 Concept of Bioethics," *Kennedy Institute of Ethics Journal*, 2007, 17(4): 279-295.

> of St. Francis of Assisi (1182-1226) with his great love toward animals, his warm sympathy for all forms of life, centuries before Rousseau's romanticism for the entire nature.[7]

This paragraph represents the first time Jahr referred formally to the concept of bioethics and, hence, it also means its origin. However, these phrases also deserve other important considerations.

Firstly, we can see that Jahr characterizes bioethics as a fundamental attitude; namely, as an *ethos*, or a way of living. In this sense, bioethics has to be developed as a part of the human character, as the affective disposition on which Aristotle writes in his *Nicomachean Ethics* when he addresses the concept of *héxis* which would be translated as *habitude* by the scholastics centuries later. The importance of this is not minor because if, according to Jahr, the concept of bioethics means a moral principle as well as a virtue, it is clear that he is talking about a new discipline which needs to be supported empirically and practically.

Secondly, Jahr redefines traditional moral obligations by extending their scope towards all extra-human nature. Thus, human beings' responsibility for their actions reaches a renewed expression that leaves the classical anthropocentrism of all previous ethics. This implies a fundamental shift in the traditional ethical conception

---

[7] Jahr, Fritz, "Bio-Ethics. Reviewing the Ethical Relations of Humans towards Animals and Plants," in *Selected Essays in Bioethics 1927-1934 Fritz Jahr*, Zentrum fur Medizinische Ethik, Bochum, November 2010, Issue 186, p. 1. Translation, Postcript and References by Hans-Martin Sass. "Bio-Ethik. Eine Umschau über die ethischen Beziehungen des Menschen zu Tier und Pflanze," in *Kosmos. Handweiser für Naturfreunde und Zentralblatt für das naturwissen-schaftliche Bildungs und Sammelwesen*, Stuttgart, 1927, 24(1): p. 2.

which results absolutely premonitory for relevant ideas that would be developed more than 50 years later such as, the imperative of responsibility of Jonas and the animal ethics of Singer and Regan, among others. In this regard, Jahr adds:

> The fact of a close interrelationship between animals protection and ethics finally is based on the reality that we not only have moral obligations towards fellow humans, but also towards animals, even against plants – in short: towards all forms of life -, so that we can speak about Bio-Ethics.[8]

Thirdly, Jahr implicitly defines bioethics as a secular and pluralistic discipline. In other words, Jahr's bioethics is pointing towards two very important conditions of possibility for current bioethics. In fact, Jahr's bioethics requires a new type of moral deliberation in order to address the new moral problems that both the new science and the new technology have brought. In this sense, and already in 1927, Jahr conceived of bioethics as a new normative and practical epistemological field.[9]

Jahr also assumes bioethics as a new moral obligation. This will imply the idea of a global bioethics whose main target should be to generate the necessary and sufficient conditions for humans to meet

---

[8] Jahr, Fritz, "The Relationship of Animal Protection and Ethics, 1928," in *Selected Essays in Bioethics 1927-1934 Fritz Jahr*, Zentrum für Medizinische Ethik, Bochum, November 2010, Issue 186, p. 1. Translation, Postcript and References by Hans-Martin Sass.

[9] In this regard, see Sass, Hans-Martin, "Poscriptum and References," in *Selected Essays in Bioethics 1927-1934 Fritz Jahr*, Zentrum für Medizinische Ethik, Bochum, November 2010, Issue 186, p. 25.

the moral compromise of respecting the life as a whole. In order to perform this purpose, Jahr formulates his Bioethical Imperative which says: "Respect every living being in principle as an end in itself and treat it, if possible, as such!"[10]

This formulation implies an epistemological and practical extension of Kantian Categorical Imperative. This does not only consider rational beings as subjects or rights but also animals and plants. Thus, the condition of possibility to be respected and considered as an end in oneself is not to be rational anymore but to be a living being.

Jahr finds the foundations for his new imperative in the Fifth Commandment "You shall not kill." He interprets this to mean not harming any kind of life, not only human life. So, there is a new moral obligation expressed in the Fifth Commandment which orders to preserve all living beings.

> When talking about moral duties, normally we mean duties towards other people in the first place. Routinely we do not consider that each person has moral duties towards oneself as well, and that those duties are of immense importance. Christian religion expressively mentions those moral duties of everyone towards oneself. That basically applies to the 5th commandment as well: 'You shall not kill.' In this sense – 'You shall

---

[10] Jahr, Fritz, "Three Studies on the Fifth Commandment, 1934," in *Selected Essays in Bioethics 1927-1934 Fritz Jahr*, Zentrum für Medizinische Ethik, Bochum, November 2010, Issue 186, p. 23. Translation, Postcript and References by Hans-Martin Sass. "Drei Studien zum 5. Gebot'" in *Kosmos. Handweiser für Naturfreunde und Zentralblatt für das naturwissen-schaftliche Bildungs und Sammelwesen,* Stuttgart, 1934, 10(1): p. 187.

> not harm or hurt anyone's body or life, rather help and support him/her in all distresses of body and life, wherever you can' – in the first place means the life of our 'neighbor.'[11]

Also, Jahr adds another argument to his imperative: human beings not only have the right to live but also they have the duty of Self-Preservation. Thus, we must care for ourselves by being responsible for our actions not only towards others but also to ourselves:

> How should these moral duties, as expressed in the 5th commandment towards one's own life, be applied in real life's practice? By not taking one's own life, by not shortening it, by not harm or endangering it, by not weakening one's own health by unchastity, excesses in eating and drinking, heavy anger, frivolous foolhardiness and daredevilry, etc.[12]

This paragraph deserves special attention since it stresses the importance of not hurting or harming others over the action of seeking the good. Therefore, the main idea that underlies this paragraph is nonmaleficence: first and foremost, not doing harm. Jahr's tacit principle is also based in the concept of the sanctity of all living beings because as Kantian moral law is inviolable, any kind of life is inviolable as well. In this sense, Jahr conceives of bioethics as

---

[11] Ibid., pp. 19-20; 10(1): p. 184.
[12] Ibid., p. 20; 10(1): p. 184.

a new ethics of virtues by redefining and extending the scope of the Golden Rule.[13]

In one of his thorough writings, Hans-Martin Sass has defined ten features of Jahr's bioethical imperative by considering it: (1) a new discipline (the bioethical imperative "needs to develop, to educate and to steward personal and collective cultural and moral attitudes and calls for new respect and responsibilities towards all forms of life"); (2) a new basic virtue ethics ("the Bioethical Imperative is based on historical and other evidence that 'compassion is an empirical established phenomenon of the human soul'"); (3) a new Golden Rule principle (as the bioethical imperative implies and stresses moral obligations among human beings and is based on compassion and love, it "cannot allow itself the Kantian luxury of just being formal"); (4) a new personal health care rule and ethics ("the bioethical imperative includes obligations towards one's own body and soul as a living being"); (5) a new public health care rule and ethics ("...fulfilling obligations towards oneself is also a duty towards others and towards public health"); (6) a new global stewardship rule and ethics ("Jahr broadens the 5th commandment into a universal rule and ethics of positively and proactively caring for the health and life of this globe as a part of a living cosmos"); (7) a new management rule and corporate ethics (the Jahr's "bioethical model of interacting forms of life in a living environment [...] would include social institutions such as those for health care"); (8)

[13] In this regard, see Sass, Hans-Martin, "Poscriptum and References," in *Selected Essays in Bioethics 1927-1934 Fritz Jahr*, Zentrum für Medizinische Ethik, Bochum, November 2010, Issue 186, p. 29.

a new terminology rule and terminological ethics ("a clear and precise terminology [...] is a priority and a precondition for clear conceptual and practical work, for communication and for cooperation and for further development"); (9) a new rule and ethics of differentiation (there must be 'different terms available for different subjects, fields, and issues" since "unclear terminology leads to unclear reasoning and acting; it is an expression of unclear thinking itself"); (10) a new interaction and integration rule and ethics ("according to Jahr, "animal ethics and social ethics are different fields, but they interact and integrate, bringing different shapes and shades of the Bioethical Imperative"). Finally, and as part of feature (10), Sass affirms that "a new field of geo-ethics is already visible" in Jarhr's bioethical imperative, since his ethics implies not only a personal commitment but also a global responsibility in order to enable "a universal, prudent and reasonable application of the Bioethical Imperative."[14]

I think it is practically impossible to refute those ten features of Jahr's bioethical imperative that Sass clearly shows us. The scope of Jahr's ideas is undoubtedly immense and represents the starting point of a new applied ethics concerned with life, health and environment based in the fact that both scientific and technological development require a new ethics, new moral deliberation, new rules

[14] Sass defines these features as "the many faces and colors of the Bioethical Imperative." See, Sass, Hans-Martin, "Poscriptum and References," in *Selected Essays in Bioethics 1927-1934 Fritz Jahr*, Zentrum für Medizinische Ethik, Bochum, November 2010, Issue 186, pp. 28-32. Another precise analysis of Jahr's bioethical imperative can be found in Sass, Hans-Martin, "Fritz Jahr's 1927 Concept of Bioethics," *Kennedy Institute of Ethics Journal* 17.4 (2007) pp. 279-295.

and procedures, and new and clear terminology in order to define and differentiate diverse fields in the realm of humanities.

Beyond the excellent analysis of Sass, I think Jahr's bioethical imperative also implies:

1. The first modern formulation of a nonmaleficence principle. Jahr's imperative implies a duty of self-preservation and, in this sense, it also entails the obligation of not harming or hurting anyone under any circumstance:

> Are the duties towards one's own life not in conflict with duties towards the neighbor? – That is not necessarily the case. On the contrary: Who fulfills one's duties towards oneself, avoids many forms of harm to other people.[15]

Jahr starts from an analysis of the Fifth Commandment by dealing with philosophical and religious tradition and, as Sass has already said, elaborating a hermeneutic "of classical old texts of various traditions and cultures" in order to base his ideas.[16] He runs a long road since the old golden rule and gospels of the New Testament until Luther, Kant and Schopenhauer's philosophies, by stressing the

---

[15] Jahr, Fritz, "Three Studies on the Fifth Commandment, 1934," in *Selected Essays in Bioethics 1927-1934 Fritz Jahr*, Zentrum für Medizinische Ethik, Bochum, November 2010, Issue 186, p. 20. Translation, Postcript and References by Hans-Martin Sass. ("Drei Studien zum 5. Gebot"" in *Kosmos. Handweiser für Naturfreunde und Zentralblatt für das naturwissen-schaftliche Bildungs und Sammelwesen,* Stuttgart, 1934, 10(1): p. 185).

[16] See, Sass, Hans-Martin, "Poscriptum and References," in *Selected Essays in Bioethics 1927-1934 Fritz Jahr*, Zentrum für Medizinische Ethik, Bochum, November 2010, Issue 186, p. 28.

importance of the sanctity of life and life's manifestations and clarifying the human duty of respecting, protecting and promoting life as a whole.

2. A prudential ethics characterized by a *phronesis* as an intellectual virtue that has to be learned with education and cultural and moral attitudes by developing the character, attitudes and dispositions of the person.[17] This point shows how Jahr's proposal is stressing a diverse and original concept of practical rationality unlike formal or intellectual ones. In this sense, Jahr thinks that his bioethics can be able to address the challenge of thinking about foundations and procedures to face the new moral issues that have emerged by virtue of new science and technology. Jahr realized the Enlightenment's failure in creating a scientific ethics. Neither Kant, with his Categorical Imperative, nor Spinoza, with his geometric ethics, were able to consolidate an ethics like physics or mathematics. However, Jahr knew that to sacrifice rationality is a luxury that ethics cannot afford. But not any rationality. According to Jahr, ethics needs a practical rationality which considers the possible consequences of human actions; namely, a practical wisdom that has to be learned by education. This emphasizes

[17] According to Aristotle, *phronesis* means a practical wisdom; namely, the knowledge that guides the human actions with criteria of morality, excellence and perfection. In this way, not all humans have *phronesis* since this has to be acquired trough education because it belongs to the group of *diano-ethical* or intellectual virtues and not to the group of ethical ones which are developed by practice. See, Aristotle, *Ethica Nicomachea (Nichomachean Ethics)*, in Mc Keon, Richard (Ed.) *The Basic Works of Aristotle*, New York, Random House, 1941, pp. 1026-1027; 1140a 24 – 1140b 30.

the disciplinary character of Jahr's bioethics; namely, the first feature that Sass has already highlighted.

3. A new ethics that considers both ends and duties as criteria of moral deliberation. We have a duty to perform: to respect all living beings as an end in itself and treat it as such, but we also have to consider further elements in order to perform that duty:

> As far as the potential realization of such moral duties towards all living beings is concerned, it might seem like utopian. But we may not ignore that moral obligations towards a living being relate to its 'needs' (Herder), respectively to its 'destiny' (Krause).[18]

Therefore, we can deduce that Jarh's bioethics represents a complementation between teleology and deontology because it enshrines a duty to perform but also implies the evaluation of consequences. Thereby, neither a tyranny of immovable principles nor an abuse of casuistry is present in Jahr's bioethical model. As Sass has said:

> The Bioethical Imperative is content-rich and balances values and life goals of living entities in their struggle

[18] Jahr, Fritz, "Three Studies on the Fifth Commandment, 1934," in *Selected Essays in Bioethics 1927-1934 Fritz Jahr*, Zentrum für Medizinische Ethik, Bochum, November 2010, Issue 186, p. 22. Translation, Postcript and References by Hans-Martin Sass. ("Drei Studien zum 5. Gebot"" in *Kosmos. Handweiser für Naturfreunde und Zentralblatt für das naturwissen-schaftliche Bildungs und Sammelwesen,* Stuttgart, 1934, 10(1): p. 187).

for life and their need for food and space and development.[19]

4. To consider seriously the concept of responsibility as a condition of possibility of any ethics. According to Jahr, bioethics is a moral attitude which implies respect and responsibilities towards all living entities. In this sense, Jahr thinks that it is no longer possible to understand the path that existence is following if people ignore the possible and also unpredictable consequences of human action which has been modified by new science and technology. Thus, Jahr is introducing the concept of responsibility in the ethical discussion long before Hans Jonas and also, with an absolutely premonitory view, he is advertising about the progress of science, especially in experimental physiology and psychology, and the necessity of ethically regulating its power in order to avoid a tyranny of humans over other living entities:

> It will always be the merit of modern natural sciences to finally have made possible an unbiased study of the world. We would not be truth-seekers today, if we would have given up the results of animal experimentation, blood research etc. On the other hand, we cannot deny that precisely these scientific triumphs

[19] Sass, Hans-Martin, "Poscriptum and References," in *Selected Essays in Bioethics 1927-1934 Fritz Jahr*, Zentrum für Medizinische Ethik, Bochum, November 2010, Issue 186, p. 26.

> of the human spirit have taken away the dominant position of the human being in the world in general.[20]

5. A sympathetic model of ethics which entails a moral and social obligation not only towards other humans but also animals and plants. Humans have the duty of extending their moral considerations to the realm of extra-human creatures, because all living beings are in constant and reciprocal interaction by establishing an interdependent relationship among each other. Also, human responsibility for animals and plants demonstrates the greatness of the human heart and it is a proof of a real moral sense that implies the presence of some of the main moral virtues such as, respect for life, benevolence, justice and compassion, among others:

> This is the issue: If we have a compassionate heart towards animals, then we will not withhold our compassion and help towards suffering humans. If someone's love is great enough to go beyond the borders of human-only and sees the sanctity even in the most miserable creature, he or she will find this sanctity as well in the most poor and lowest fellow human, will hold it high and will not reduce it to class

[20] Jahr, Fritz, "Bio-Ethics. Reviewing the Ethical Relations of Humans towards Animals and Plants," in *Selected Essays in Bioethics 1927-1934 Fritz Jahr*, Zentrum für Medizinische Ethik, Bochum, November 2010, Issue 186, p. 1. Translation, Postcript and References by Hans-Martin Sass. ("Bio-Ethik. Eine Umschau über die ethischen Beziehungen des Menschen zu Tier und Pflanze," in *Kosmos. Handweiser für Naturfreunde und Zentralblatt für das naturwissen-schaftliche Bildungs und Sammelwesen,* Stuttgart, 1927, 24(1): p. 2).

> of society, interest group, one party or what else may be considered. On the other hand, senseless cruelty towards animals is an indication of an unrefined character becoming dangerous towards the human environment as well.[21]

This point certainty reinforces Jahr's figure as a pioneer not only of bioethics but also of animal and environmental ethics. His imperative also entails an extension of Kantian moral duty by transcending the anthropocentric frontiers of traditional ethics since every living entity on the earth is worthy of respect and moral consideration.

6. To recognize all living beings as worthy of respect:

> The fact of close interrelationship between animal protection and ethics finally is based on the reality that we not only have moral obligations towards fellow humans, but also towards animals, even against plants – in short: towards all forms of life – , so that we can speak about 'Bio-Ethics.'[22]

---

[21] Jahr, Fritz, "The Relationship of Animal Protection and Ethics, 1928," in *Selected Essays in Bioethics 1927-1934 Fritz Jahr*, Zentrum für Medizinische Ethik, Bochum, November 2010, Issue 186, p. 5. Translation, Postcript and References by Hans-Martin Sass. ("Tierschuzt and Ethik," in *Aufsatze zur Bioethik 1927-1928 Fritz Jahr*. Nachwort und Nachweise von Hans-Martin Sass, Zentrum für Medizinische Ethik, Bochum, Dezember 2010, Issue 187, p. 9).

[22] Ibid., p. 6.

Even though Jahr never mentioned it explicitly, he is tacitly talking about extending the human right to be respected to animals and plants:

> [...] They all, plants and animals, also humans, have similar rights, but not Equal Right, depending on the requirements for reaching their specific destiny.[23]

However, I have to emphasize that this extension is not complete. Jahr is not proposing to treat animals and plants as humans. He thinks that we should respect any kind of life by distinguishing their ontological nature: "We owe justice to humans; mildness and mercy towards all living beings, capable of having a benefit from that."[24] This can be considered as a first argument to sustain the concept of *sentience* which Peter Singer addresses in his famous book *Animal Liberation* in 1975.

7. A public Ethics because Jahr not only emphasizes the binding character of not doing harm but also its larger scope:

---

[23] Jahr, Fritz, "Bio-Ethics. Reviewing the Ethical Relations of Humans towards Animals and Plants," in *Selected Essays in Bioethics 1927-1934 Fritz Jahr*, Zentrum fur Medizinische Ethik, Bochum, November 2010, Issue 186, p. 2. Translation, Postcript and References by Hans-Martin Sass. "Bio-Ethik. Eine Umschau über die ethischen Beziehungen des Menschen zu Tier und Pflanze," in *Kosmos. Handweiser für Naturfreunde und Zentralblatt für das naturwissen-schaftliche Bildungs und Sammelwesen,* Stuttgart, 1927, 24(1): p. 3.

[24] Jahr, Fritz, "Three Studies on the Fifth Commandment, 1934," in *Selected Essays in Bioethics 1927-1934 Fritz Jahr*, Zentrum für Medizinische Ethik, Bochum, November 2010, Issue 186, p. 21. Translation, Postcript and References by Hans-Martin Sass. "Drei Studien zum 5. Gebot"" in *Kosmos. Handweiser für Naturfreunde und Zentralblatt für das naturwissen-schaftliche Bildungs und Sammelwesen,* Stuttgart, 1934, 10(1): p. 186.

> Who, however, protects one's own life in this respect, fulfills one's duty also towards the community. [...] And thus does not only harm oneself, but one's family as well, one's offsprings, one's country, one's race. And again: if one protects oneself in this regard against harm, one does, at the same time, good to one's neighbor, actually to one's entire country.[25]

According to this paragraph, the global meaning of Jahr's bioethics as well as its civic and public character is clear. We are in front of a dialogical ethics where moral truth is not the privilege of an individual consciousness but an argumentative community whose decisions might affect the whole of society. This systemic feature of Jahr's bioethics was absolutely visionary for the current discipline and it would be very helpful and useful for its further development and better understanding if bioethicists would seriously consider Jahr's work which was absolutely original and has undoubtedly inaugurated the discipline that we know today as bioethics.

The historical neglect of Jahr's figure has been as unfair as it has been baffling. It is practically impossible to find references to Jahr in bioethical literature, even in books authored by bioethicists of recognized prestige and reputation, and it is also really disappointing to read books on the history and origins of bioethics that do not consider its real founder at all. In this sense, the work of Hans-

[25] Ibid., p. 20; 10(1): p. 185.

Martin Sass for recuperating Jahr's ideas constitutes an extremely valuable enterprise.
Obviously, Jahr's bioethics is not the same as that which we know today. My goal has just been to demonstrate that his ideas represent the first guidelines of bioethics and bioethical principlism. Indeed, Jahr tacitly includes in his concept of bioethics some important principles such as autonomy, social justice and, at that time, a completely new idea of nonmaleficence. In this sense, Jahr, beyond being the creator of the term and concept "bioethics," has designed the first foundations and keys of this discipline, by substantially collaborating with its theoretical configuration. For all these reasons, and due to his brilliant, advanced and precursory thoughts, Jahr deserves a prominent place in the history of bioethics.

## I.2. Medical Ethics' Tradition

As Albert Jonsen has said, "bioethics did not begin with a Big Bang."[26] Beyond the essential contribution of Jahr, several milestones, occurring between 1803 and 1971, can be considered as potential factors that progressively originated interest and concern about the relationships between science, medicine and ethics. Gradually and increasingly, the notorious advances and progress of science and technology generated new moral problems whose complexity could not be addressed by a traditional moral reflection. The necessity for new systematic guidelines was demonstrated.

[26] Jonsen, Albert R., *The Birth of Bioethics*, New York, Oxford University Press, 1998, p. 3.

However, bioethics had to perambulate a long road before becoming a discipline yet.

In 1803, Thomas Percival, an English physician, published his book *Medical Ethics*. It was the first work in history that formally addressed that issue. Percival took diverse elements from traditional virtues, such as rectitude, respect and compromise, and applied them to the medical profession. In fact, the main goal of Percival's book was to regulate the relationships between physicians and surgeons in England by stressing the importance of professional duties, civil responsiveness, public trust and discipline.[27] However, one of the most important reasons that Percival had to write his book was the huge social transformation made possible by the industrial revolution, whose effects were already reaching medical practice because "in Britain's laissez-faire free-market economy, doctors were tempted to adopt entrepreneurial attitudes, operating according to the law of 'let the buyer beware.'"[28]

Percival provided the first theoretical and procedural guidelines in order to shape a new epistemological and disciplinary field, based in social ethics principles. His starting point was to consider that medicine, as a profession of social impact, must be performed with excellence in order to cure and reinforce the physicians' role in society as well as to reach a level of professional reliability. Thus, in those days, he started configuring an epistemological frame that conceived of physicians as professionals who precisely professed

---

[27] Post, Stephen G., *Encyclopedia of Bioethics*, 3rd Edition, Macmillan Reference USA, 2004, pp.1595-96.

[28] Ibid.

their activity by publicly performing it. In other words, a physician became a person who was devoted to his profession and became publicly recognized as such.[29] Jonsen considered this last point quite important:

> […] Physicians must define their place in society. They must show themselves as worthy of social trust and deserving of social authority and reward. This "social ethics," hardly noted in the ancient medical world, began to assume importance during the Middle Ages, as medicine was being taught in universities, guilds and colleges were being established, and civic authorities were taking notice of the dangers of untrained practitioners. The marks of the profession began to appear: the privilege to educate, examine, license, and discipline their members, and the tacit pledge of public service.[30]

By virtue of its professional feature, medicine entails public and institutional responsibility both to the whole society and to those who receive the product of the profession; that is, healing. Thereby, with Percival's Code medicine starts to be considered not only as a practice but also as a public commitment that demands the highest excellence in the executed action. In other words, physicians should be prepared to demand of themselves high quality and training standards as well as to be aware of their responsibility for

[29] Percival, Thomas, *Medical Ethics: or, a Code of Institutes and Precepts, Adapted to the Professional Conduct of Physicians and Surgeons*, London, S. Russell, 1803.
[30] Jonsen, Albert R., *The Birth of Bioethics*, New York, Oxford University Press, 1998, p. 7.

consequences arising from their actions in order to define their role in society and achieve public trust.

It was not until the mideighteenth century that Percival's guidelines acquired more importance and their scope became extended by radically influencing the American Medical Association's (AMA) Code, which was established in 1847 in order "to reform medical education and to improve the ethics of physicians."[31] Evidently, both medicine as a professional discipline and physicians as moral agencies needed to improve. In this sense, AMA entailed awareness about the medical teaching system's lacks not only from an epistemological point of view but also from an ethical one. AMA understood that physicians were only not doctors or healing machines by dealing with patients but humans who must not only be knowledgable about science but also about morality. Although a new kind of medicine was arising, its scientific character was still stressed over the ethical one. Jonsen says:

> The Code was largely based on Percival's *Medical Ethics*, as adapted to American needs and tastes. One chapter, reflecting the American scene, repudiated quackery, forbade advertising, and prohibited consultation with doctors "whose practice is based on an exclusive dogma, to the rejection of the accumulated experience of the profession, and of the aids actually furnished by anatomy, physiology, pathology and organic chemistry. Those words [...] banished from

[31] Post, Stephen G., *Encyclopedia of Bioethics*, 3rd Edition, Macmillan Reference USA, 2004, p. 1597.

> "the regular profession" all doctors who practiced forms of "sectarian" medicine, such as homeopathy, naturopathy, and hydropathy.[32]

The Code represented an effort to give medicine several procedural rules in order to professionalize it. Also, the Code specified medical virtues and orientated physicians' behavior by representing one of the first modern expressions of an applied ethics, since its main goals were related to determining and delimitating medical responsibilities as well as rights and duties in medical practice. In this way, the Code stressed traditional moral categories attributed to physicians and based on the Hippocratic Oath, such as decorum, gentleness, pleasantness, discretion and firmness, among others.
The Code was revised in 1903 by acquiring the name of "Principles of Medical Ethics." Despite a further intervention (1912) the "principles" remained the same until 1957 when they were reduced to ten statements which finally became only seven in 1966. Briefly, the principles were stated as follows 1. *To respect the rights of patients*. We can consider it as a principle of proto-autonomy since it recognizes the patient as an active and important moral agency, and it makes the physician-patient's relationship more horizontal. Although both limits of self-determination and conditions of possibility for a free and informed decision were not well defined yet, we may understand this principle as a precedent of the current

[32] Jonsen, Albert R., *The Birth of Bioethics*, New York, Oxford University Press, 1998, p. 7.

bioethical principle of respect for autonomy.[33] 2. *To consider patients' skills* by involving their opinions and concerns in the decision-making process. This principle aimed to legitimize patients as valid interlocutors despite such *recognition used to be merely formal* and encountered several problems of application in practice. This, since it was not clear (it is still not clear) whether or not the patient can assign personal values to the benefits and risks of intervention. 3. *To accept the discipline of the profession*. This implied awareness of special and specific responsibilities of medical practice. 4. *To assume own limitations and consult if necessary*. This principle demystified the physician's figure as an infallible person who was close to perfection and completely far from error. 5. *To respect the professional secret's doctrine and not to tell confidences*. Today, this principle seems rigid because in the light of current bioethical principlism, the dogmatic act of never telling a confidence may imply maleficent consequences such as to undermine the good of patients. 6. *To be good citizens* by reinforcing and emphasizing the public character of medicine and the social scope of *ars medica*. 7. *To maintain professional independence* in order to exercise medicine and make decisions free of external coercion such as to receiving incomes other than medical services.[34]

---

[33] However, several questions were still not addressed: Can the patient actually communicate a choice? Can the patient understand what doctors are saying? Is the patient able to understand information rationally and logically? Is the patient's decision-making capacity stable over time? (See, Jones, Roger C., Holden, Timothy, "A Guide to Assessing Decision Making Capacity" in *Cleveland Clinic Journal of Medicine*, vol 71, 12, December 2004, p. 973.).

[34] See, Baker, Robert et al., *The Codification of Medical Morality*, vol. 1 and Baker, Robert (ed.), *The Codification of Medical Morality*, vol. 2, Dordrecht/Boston, Kluwer Academic Publishers, 1995.

Certainly, medical ethics became a procedural code that established 'behavioral rules' whose foundation was the historical medical tradition. Thus, and despite its advances, the Code still did not contemplate big new challenges which medicine had to confront due to scientific and technological development.

Disciplinary, medical ethics constitutes a historical precedent of bioethics. Both are applied ethics and seek to address and resolve problems related to medical practice. We will see later that medical ethics lacks some key attributes that bioethics does own, especially since traditional medical ethics is still inspired by Hippocratic precepts and imposes a medical model based in a paternalistic attitude towards patients. However, as an applied ethics, medical ethics does imply a new hermeneutic of moral problems since it has been able to acknowledge their particular nature and specific complexity which, as such, must be also addressed with specific procedures.

However, the challenges facing medical ethics are not exactly the same as bioethics. Indeed, the procedural and theoretical scope of medical ethics is not as wide as bioethics'. This has a larger 'operative field' as medical ethics moves within the context of the health care profession by referring specifically to the physician-patient relationship. According to Pellegrino:

> [...]The ethics of medicine should be based in the nature of the medical relationship, that is, in a philosophy *of* medicine [...] the obligations specific to physicians arise from the special features of the

> personal relationship between the person who is ill and the person the ill person seeks for help. The resulting relationship has certain features that give it a special character that generates special mutual moral duties.[35]

This physician-patient relationship or "clinical encounter," as Pellegrino calls it, represents the source of moral, existential, experiential and phenomenological aspects of the medical profession. In this way, the clinical encounter does not only imply the field on which a medical ethics must work, but also it means the justification of medicine itself. Pellegrino has argued that there are three essential phenomena of the clinical encounter that can help to clarify what makes medicine is what it is:

> 1) The existential fact of illness or disease, 2) the act of promise or profession by the physician who offers to help the patient caught in the predicament of illness, and 3) the act of medicine – making the technically right and the morally good decision that best serves the needs of the sick person as grasped by that person and her physician.[36]

On this view, the main goal of the clinical encounter is the good of the patient, which entails "a right and good healing and helping act."

---

[35] Pellegrino, Edmund, "From Medical Ethics to a Moral Philosophy of the Profession," in Walter, Jennifer K., and Klein, Eran P. (editors), *The Story of Bioethics*, Washington, DC, Georgetown University Press, 2003, p. 5.
[36] Ibid., p. 6.

Thereby, and in order to achieve such good, a real medical ethics should be based on virtues and duties such as, "fidelity, trust, benevolence, truth telling, intellectual honesty, humility, courage, suppression of self-interest," among others.[37]
Although medical ethics admits different models, Pellegrino's approach is one of the most widely accepted since it summarizes the universally agreed *telos* of medical ethics. In short, these could be stated as follows:

- Theoretically, medical ethics is based on a virtue ethics that demands the excellence of physicians and trust of the patient.
- Procedurally, medical ethics is based on the clinical encounter between the physician and the patient. This encounter entails the starting point of rights and obligations of medical *praxis*.
- The physician-patient relationship is not an event but a process.
- Essentially, the benefit of the patient is always the medical ethics' *telos*.

However, medical ethics is not bioethics. Indeed, medical ethics has been virtually replaced by the new discipline in the procedural field. The reason is as clear as it is irrefutable: medical ethics can only be considered as a precedent of bioethics since both its foundations and procedures are not enough to make decisions about the most complex problems that have arisen in the medical field because of

[37] Ibid., p. 7.

cientific progress and technological empowerment. Just to give the readers an overview of its shortcomings, I could say that the format of traditional medical ethics:

- Does not specify what the objective patient's good is.
- Does not give concrete procedures to determine that good.
- Implies that the patient's good is a determination of the physician by virtue of his alleged epistemological superiority.
- Is procedural and excessively focused on the practical realm. However, the concept of good *praxis* is defined from what physicians think good *praxis* means.
- Is still vertical and quite paternalistic. This means that medical ethics entails a subjective, casuistic, dogmatic and deontological code. It is subjective because despite most of the decisions being made by considering the patient's good and by taking into consideration his/her wellness, those decisions mostly depend on an excessively epistemological perspective; that is, they depend on professional considerations properly related to clinical and technical abilities. It is casuistic because medical ethics consider very general and common sense principles. Those do not represent real theoretical and procedural guidelines to address moral deliberation with certain possibilities of success. Thereby, decision-making is developed from the particular case since general principles lack a sufficient foundation to conduct the resolution of particular moral dilemmas. These general moral rules of

medical ethics conflict by forcing a careful distinction of the case to which those rules have to be applied. Therefore, the definition of what is right and wrong is obtained from the specific case which should show the general rules to apply, and also the procedure becomes too inductive and, precisely because of that, it does not provide any certainty that in the future the same decision will be made for a similar case.

Medical ethics has its basis in Western philosophical tradition. Diverse ethical theories converge in its foundations. This point that seems to be a fortress is also a weakness. Although medical ethics pull out the best from practically all Western ethical theories, this eclecticism often means a clash of principles and moral criteria which, in theory, are equivalent.[38] Diversity of foundations in medical ethics entails not only conflict but also contradiction between theoretical guidelines that are too general and therefore too vague. Medical ethics does not recognize a basic principle of moral deliberation: we always have to take into account that a general ethical theory hardly ever fits in a moral problem which always implies a particular conflict; that is, a specific case.

Pellegrino has recognized this problem by offering his own point of view and his own possible solution. He thinks that a medical ethics should be based on natural aspects of the clinical relationship. In this

---

[38] A historical overview of ethical theories and medical ethics shows how several and diverse ethical conceptions are at the basis of medical ethics. We can find aspects of Virtues Ehics, Christian Ethics, Natural Law Theories, Social Contract Theories, Kantian Ethics, Utilitarianism, among others. See: Pence, Gregory E., *Classic Cases in Medical Ethics*, New York, Mc Graw Hill, 2004, pp. 10-21.

way, the doctor-patient relation must be based in a "philosophy *of* medicine" whose foundations arise from "the special features of the personal relationship between the person who is ill and the person the ill person seeks for help."[39] That does not mean, according to Pellegrino, that medical ethics dispense with a general ethics foundation. However, those general principles, ends and duties are not coming from a static set of values but from the nature of the human relationship involved in the clinical encounter. In this sense, Pellegrino thinks that the basis of a medical ethics must be obtained from "the existential, experiential, and phenomenological aspects" strongly related to the essential features of any medical relationship.[40]

In sum, we could say that medical ethics constitutes a kind of applied ethics as bioethics is, although that is not necessarily focused on specific aspects arisen from technological development. Medical ethics is rather a set of procedural standards that seek to regulate Pellegrino's "clinical encounter" as well as physicians' behavior.[41] Medical ethics' main goal is to regulate the professional conduct of physicians in order to benefit the patient. Thus, its scope is more limited and relative than bioethics.

---

[39] Pellegrino, Edmund, "From Medical Ethics to a Moral Philosophy of the Profession," in Walter, Jennifer K., and Klein, Eran P. (editors), *The Story of Bioethics*, Washington, DC, Georgetown University Press, 2003, p. 5.

[40] Ibid., pp. 5-6.

[41] Ibid., p. 7. According to Pellegrino "clinical encounter" means the clinical relationship between physician and patient by always seeking "the good of the patient or, in more clinical terms, a right and good healing and helping act."

## I.3. Biotechnological Achievements: New Challenges and New Perils

The techno-scientific development and all its implications to life, as a whole, have meant a fundamental milestone in the emergence of bioethics. Indeed, bioethics is a consequence of modern technology's empowerment and presents, in relation to that historical event, new ways of asking about the relationship between human beings and technology in an era deeply influenced by the modified character of human action.

Technology of the new era does not only consist of large machinery, and mega systems or mega structures for production purposes. It affects and modifies, above all, the daily interaction between humans and the world, namely from that relationship which is established between the subject and its sphere of existence, which is conceived as a technological field, like a new world, a new dimension, apparently divergent of human morality.

The ethics/technology imbrication appears in contemporary times, crossed by a totally novel aspect: the modification of human action that leads to technological progress. This modification also touches upon the immediate field of influence of the human being, which also would have become fractured, broken up and disfigured from the technological colonization that reaches all levels of networks and relationships. Human beings live technologically, which means that technology is not something that occurs outside, on the contrary, it is practically no longer possible to live without it. The question then, is whether this new relationship is likely to be modulated ethically, without any of those attempts becoming merely cosmetic or strategic as a way of providing impunity to the power of technology.

In this sense, biotechnology acquires an ethical connotation at this time since it means a phenomenon which is essentially social, that is, inter-subjective. Biotechnology does not belong to a particular individual but all society. Indeed, biotechnology seeks to deploy in time and space because this expansion constitutes its condition of ontological possibility. Without expansion, without globalization, biotechnology is nothing. For this reason, biotechnology should be addressed from a public policies' perspective where bioethics plays a principal role since biotechnology, despite its new possibilities and new horizons, also threatens not only the future of this or that individual but the entire social collective.

Biotechnology raises new challenges to bioethics because it has opened an abyss between what human beings can do and what they can anticipate. Biotechnology's achievements entail a new relationship between individuals and technological possibilities. This is no longer an instrumental relation between subject and object since everything human beings used to do with technology, by seeking our wellness based in a harmonious use of technological resources, have turned into a connection that is only justified through a radical idea of progress which is essentially linked to the impulse of intervening in the biological life.

Biotechnological discoveries and scientific developments are reciprocally potentiated. At the present time, the dimension of actions, or rather, the possibilities of human action are totally new. Never before in the history of mankind has the mentality that underlies the technological era been observed, which is seen in the quite inquisitive attitude of human beings towards the entities of the world. The predominant mode of being is now a technological way of being, supported and strengthened by the works that have arisen from the manufacturing ability of *homo technicus*. The blind confidence of the individual in his ability to make things causes his biotechnology to revert on himself. It is the culmination of his will of power which leads to his own submission to the techno-scientific paradigm of modern times.

This submission is the result of what Jonas has called the "idea of progress" which is inherent in biotechnology, from which a circular relationship is consolidated between means and ends, which eventually disrupts the balance between human needs and the instruments that are manufactured to satisfy them. This circular relationship means that certain ends that human beings have always sought are satisfied better, especially with the new means created by technology. However, these new means push the proliferation of new needs, and these in turn cause the production of other increasingly more sophisticated instruments, to account for them.

Because of this steady circular relationship which certainly divides the balance outlined above, innovation is nurtured in this relationship and begins to be sought permanently and deliberately. From this phenomenon, which is characteristic of biotechnology, Jonas adds to his reflection the fact of the global scope of these innovations: each time they appear, they are rapidly disseminated throughout the world.

However, according to Jonas, the most serious matter is that this progress creates a dynamic that overpowers human will and which generates a kind of technological imperative, which requires putting into practice everything that seems possible in theory. Thus, the possibility of authentic freedom is vanished. Only a permanent progress remains, even against our own discretion and consideration. This development is so remarkable that it occurs in a succession of stages which also reflects the progress of science: from mechanics to chemistry, then electrodynamics, then to nuclear physics, and finally to biotechnology. The latter provides, to Jonas, a rare novelty: from advanced biological knowledge, humans can manipulate life and become, themselves, a new object of technology.[42]

By intervening and manipulating life, that is, its genetic codes, the scientist modifies its direction and takes control of it. From this point of view, it is possible to say that genetic manipulation represents the complete triumph of rationality in its control over nature and the human being, resulting in a total lack of meaning and content.

Therefore, biotechnology, which bases itself on a criterion of utility, of economics, of the merely possible, which focuses on production and in production only and not on other legitimate aims, turns the existence of the human being into a contradiction. Science and technology are distorted to the point where they do not receive guidance from the essential space in which human beings exist; there they are not conducted from the standpoint of responsibility

[42] Jonas, Hans, *Das Prinzip Veranwortung: Versuchi einer Ethic für die Tecnologische Zivilisation*, Francfort am Main, Insel Verlag, 1988, p. 43.

towards life, or there where they have lost their horizon of sense, converting themselves, beforehand, into a theory and a praxis that have no vision and are unable to foresee the consequences of their actions. One could say, then, that the closure of the sphere of meaning is the very closure of the possibility of a better life since enhancement does not necessarily mean improvement.

With the current phenomenon of biotechnological intervention, we are witnessing the manipulation and provocation of the very source, where nature serves as a platform for human dwelling. That is, that from a techno-mechanicist perspective, the current understanding we have of life is that of an unprecedented space of domain and calculation. In fact, science and technology are not the problem but rather the way that they are received and understood, that is, the relationship that we have established with them. This new technological possibility is also a new kind of violence against life, based on precise calculation and determination, which converts us, as Nietzsche said, into an animal without metaphors or, in new words, into an individual reduced to the literalness of a complete sequence of genetic instructions, thanks to that knowledge too exactly how we're made and how it works in pursuit of the calculation, and for the sake of planning and the exact order of all things. This subject as an animal without metaphors, as a *subjectum* who has put nature and himself before himself, impedes to experience a relationship with the world understood as the sphere of existence.

From these considerations, biotechnological problems are also bioethical problems. In fact, bioethics would never have existed if biotechnology had not emerged before by developing a set of technical procedures to manipulate, intervene and even modify biological systems. In the following, I will enumerate diverse biotechnological achievements that show clearly how much technology has advanced and how close its relation to bioethics is or, in other words, why bioethics must address moral problems arisen from biotechnological development. As we will see, the task of bioethics is not at all easy, since biotechnological advances have been so fast and continual that it seems almost impossible to give an account of all of them. My narration will be neutral by avoiding punishing biotechnology itself. However, most of biotechnological products and effects are no longer science fiction, they are already real and bioethics should pay special attention to them as such.

*Cloning*:[43] From the Greek work *klon* (twig), cloning has different possible definitions. First, it could be defined as a means of asexual reproduction, in which there is no need of meiosis and fertilization (both of them are basic processes of almost all sexual reproduction).
Another definition is the "transplantation of a nucleus from a cell into an ovum."[44] This transplantation process is done by removing the chromosomal genetic information from an oocyte and "fertilizing" with it a diploid cell. This process is carried out instead of fertilizing a haploid oocyte with a haploid sperm.
Finally, the most common and broad of definitions for cloning is simply "making a genetic copy." That genetic identity does not

[43] For full reference, refer to Encyclopedia of Bioethics, 3rd Edition, 2004, pp. 447-466.
[44] Ibid., p. 448.

equal phenotypic identity, due either to epigenetic or environmental effects[45]. Another source of difference may also be the mutation in the DNA in nuclear chromosomes or mitochondria.

There are numerous procedures used for cloning mammals of which two are the most common ones. The first is concerned with making identical copies of embryos from embryonic cells; the second one is used to create embryos with identical nuclear DNA from cells of embryos, fetuses, young animals and adult cells.[46]

Cloning technology has certain potential inherent to its own nature and it is not only applied to produce more offspring but also to obtain basic biological information that can be used in other areas, such as research on birth defects, cancer and other diseases.

Among the most relevant applications of cloning we can find: making genetic copies of outstanding agricultural animals; making more useful transgenic technology; and therapeutic cloning to produce tissue and organ replacement parts in humans.[47]

Due to the large number of possibilities that cloning technology has opened, there are several related ethical issues to consider and, in this sense, debate is abundant. On one hand, there are supporters of cloning, who assert that this technology, once perfected, will be of great assistance to humans. Their arguments are mostly focused on cloning's benefits to enhance the quality of human life. According to them, this is a solid moral ground to base and support cloning's

---

[45] "Effects due to genes that vary from organism to organism due to random chance, therefore, cannot ever be predicted exactly." Ibid., p. 448.

[46] Ibid., p.449. For full in-depth procedures refer to pages 450-51.

[47] Full ethical debate can be found in Encyclopedia of Bioethics, 3rd Edition, 2004, pp. 451-52

development. On the other hand, detractors such as the Catholic Church insist that human cloning (in particular) is not a natural means of creating life, by condemning it for its "anti-natural" ways. These criticisms are mostly based on the teachings and dogmas of the Catholic Church, by questioning the inherent value of "cloned life."

Debate also exists around the quality of cloned life by especially considering the following statement:

> Animal offspring derived from *in vitro* fertilization or long-term *in vitro* culture of embryos have a much higher incidence of abnormalities that with normal reproduction.[48]

Then, is cloning right by considering the relatively high risk of abnormal children?

*Stem cells*:[49] Embryonic stem cells were first grown in culture in 1998 by James Thomson at the University of Wisconsin. He reported to the journal *Science* that "such human embryonic stem cells formed a wide variety of recognizable tissue when planted into mice."[50]

There are two major types of stem cells: embryonic stem-cells, which are isolated from the inner cell mass of blastocysts, and adult stem-cells, which can be found in several tissues. In a

---

[48] Encyclopedia of Bioethics, 3rd Edition, 2004, p. 453.
[49] For full reference, refer to the Encyclopedia of Bioethics, 3rd Edition, pp. 722-731
[50] Ibid., p. 722.

developing embryo, stem cells can differentiate into all the specialized cells, but they also maintain the normal turnover of regenerative organs, such as blood, skin, or intestinal tissues.[51] They attracted immediate attention from the scientific community because of their ability to divide through mitosis and diversify into different and specialized cell types. Also, they can self-renew to produce even more stem-cells.

Among their other abilities, they seem to be able to "trigger cell regeneration" and "colonize damaged tissue," by repairing *in situ*. This all is deemed as a promising means of halting or even curing many diseases such as Alzheimer's disease, spinal cord injury, stroke, burns, heart disease, diabetes, osteoarthritis, and rheumatoid arthritis.[52] Some people even speak about the possibility of "immortality."[53]

Such technology also entails diverse ethical concerns which have raised controversial and very important issues. Many of these issues are related to the way these stem cells are obtained (currently, they are obtained from adults, umbilical cord blood and fetal and embryonic tissue). General consensus is that embryos are the best source of stem cells for therapeutic purposes. However, this consensus is subject to change as research develops and ethical questions increase: Should embryos or fetuses be deliberately produced as a means of obtaining stem cells? Who gives consent when using embryonic or fetal tissue? (Certainly fetuses cannot

[51] http://stemcells.nih.gov/info/basics/basics1.asp
[52] Ibid.
[53] Encyclopedia of Bioethics, 3rd Edition, 2004, p.723.

consent). Should we desire, given the chance, immortality? How does that affect our conceptions of the basics of human nature?

*Genetic Manipulation/Engineering:*[54]Also known as "Genetic Engineering" or "Genetic Modification," this concept refers to the direct human manipulation of the genome of any kind of organisms (humans, animals, plants).

Genetic Manipulation involves the introduction of recombinant DNA (rDNA). This technology uses enzymes to cut and paste together DNA sequences of interest. The recombined DNA sequences can be placed into vehicles called vectors that ferry the DNA into a suitable host cell where it can be copied or expressed) or synthetic genes into said organism in order to give it a desired phenotype.[55]

When genetic material from another species is added to the host organism, we can then say it is a "transgenic" organism; when genetic material is added from the same species the resulting organism is called cisgenic.[56]

This technology allows a wide range of possibilities, especially when applied on humans. By modifying our inherited genetic information (or animals') we can prevent genetic diseases, enhance intelligence and health, enable parents to have kids genetically related to them (in other circumstances, kids would not be able to), reduce social costs of genetic diseases, benefit the human gene pool

---

[54] Ibid., pp. 959-966.

[55] http://www.genome.gov/Glossary/index.cfm?id=173, from the National Institute of Health web resources.

[56] http://www.genome.gov/Glossary/index.cfm?id=199.

by promoting good genes and eradicating bad genes, among other uses. All these reasons are presented by supporters of Genetic Manipulation.[57]

On the contrary, detractors respond by pointing out interesting arguments, such as:[58]

1. Social injustices that might be created by modifying some individuals and some not by posibilitating another form of discrimination.
2. Humans should not "play god," because we lack the wisdom and authority to design life.
3. Heath-care resources could be better spent on other areas.
4. Medical dangers associated with the practice of genetic engineering.

Directly related to genetic engineering we have another, more precise concept:

*Genetic Enhancement*:[59] It is generally understood as the use of genetic engineering aimed at "improving the quality of the human genome."[60] It is said to contrast with "Genetic Therapy" which entails using genetic engineering for "fixing" defective genes or inserting "corrected" genes as means of therapy. However, there is

[57] Encyclopedia of Bioethics, 3rd Edition, 2004, p. 963.
[58] Ibid.
[59] For full reference, see: Encyclopedia of Bioethics, 3rd Edition, 2004, p. 963.
[60] Ibid., p. 978.

no clear difference and consensus of what would constitute enhancement and what would be therapy.

Genetic Enhancement is directly related to the so-called "Eugenics" movement – from Greek *Eu* (good or well) with added suffix *genēs* (born, generation) – which has been one of the most controversial subjects in the scientific community during the past century. The term was first coined by Sir Francis Galton in 1883 to describe the efforts that could be done in deliberate reproductive control on human beings (analogous to the deliberate reproduction used in agricultural sciences at those years) and its benefits. Since then, the rise of Nazism and their appropriation of the term, related to those infamous experiments they justified as "research," have tainted eugenics with a negative connotation. Decades later, the mapping of the human genome, which started during the 1990's and ended the year 2003, gave new life to the eugenics movement, as people started recognizing its possibilities for beneficial individual therapies used freely by individuals and not imposed by the State. The main aim is then to *improve* the lifetime of *future* individuals who would otherwise face genetic deficiencies and/or disadvantages. As with any technological development, ethical issues arise: Who should decide which are and which are not desirable eugenic goals? Should this power change future human beings and shape them as we see fit? Will the differences created be fair? Who should get access to enhancement of their genes?

*Transgenics*:[61] Related to Genetic Engineering we find the concept of "Transgenesis." According to the Encyclopedia of Genetics, transgenic organisms are "species in which the genome has been modified by the insertion of genes obtained from another species."[62] During the late 1970's and 1980's "scientists invented procedures for combining the DNA of species as distantly related as plant and animals."[63] These procedures are similar to gene therapy (part of genetic engineering) since both of them change cells for specific purposes.

The goal of transgenesis is to create a whole new modified living organism by incorporating transgene into all cells of the mature organism, including the germ cells. In that way it can transfer the genetic information when it reproduces.

The first animal transgenic transformation was possible in 1978 when yeast cells were transformed with the insertion of foreign DNA. Soon after, in 1979, mouse cells would follow the same process.

Transgenic plants cells prove to be of greater difficulty due to their larger cell walls, compared to animal cells. Thus, some processes for transgenesis such as "microinjection" and "biolistics" are slower and harder to perform. A wide variety of transgenic plants have been designed for agricultural use, these we know as genetically modified food. A slowly ripening type of tomato was the first of these types of food to be marketed. Then corn, cotton, soybeans and potatoes were

[61] Ness, Bryan D., Encyclopedia of Genetics, Revised Edition, New Jersey, Salem Press Inc., 2004, pp.739 – 742.
[62] Ibid., p. 326.
[63] Ibid., p. 739.

genetically transformed for their enhancement; soon other crops would be genetically enhanced as well and were made available at the market.

Transgenesis has also been criticized by the global community: manipulation of life, hidden health risks, cruel violation to animal rights, and environmental issues, among others. All of these issues and many others pose ethical quandaries that have been attended and will continue being attended as technology advances.

*Bio-informatic*: With biotechnology and semiconductor's developments, scientists are now able to create something like "micro laboratories" that can perform thousands of chemical reactions simultaneously, just like traditional silicon computer chips do, using systems of biologically derived molecules (some biochips can be electronic), such as DNA and proteins, to perform a computer's task: storing, retrieving, and processing data.[64] Simply put, this means that now we can pack much more information in much less space, process it and store it; this means an increase in processing power, too.

This is one of the many advances in biotechnology, which focuses its efforts on "the application of recombinant DNA technology to the development of specific products and procedures."[65] Genetic engineering has made possible the emulation of computer processes without the use of silicon-based chips, which supposes a bright future for the informatics world. And although the development of

[64] http://willson.cm.utexas.edu/Research/Sub_Files/Biochip/index.php, University of Texas.
[65] Encyclopedia of Genetics, Revised Edition, p. 326.

this technology is rudimentary, scientists are already starting to imagine possible uses for all the potential it holds.
Bioinformatics could be defined as a branch of technology that focuses on data storage and usage in biotechnology. Advances are always bringing more and more information that needs to be processed, stored and made available for future reference. In this specific aspect, bioinformatics plays an important role "in relation to research and infrastructure for biotechnology."[66]
Once again, all this potential is not exempt from criticism. Advances in biotechnology and especially in bioinformatics and biochips, propose interesting ethical issues that should be addressed. The most important of questions seems to be the following: What uses are we giving to this technology and why? All the possibilities are open.

Certainly, all these new discoveries and technologies have opened new possibilities for science but also new challenges for bioethics. All bioetechnological achievements mean new possibilities of therapy but also imply a voracious appetite for enhancing life and doing everything that seems possible to in theory. Complex issues, such as commercial eugenics, genetic discrimination and bioterrorism, among others, are no longer fiction and have become into a disturbing actuality. Technology has a double face since it is hope and peril at the same time. This ambiguity refutes the alleged neutrality of technology. This is not neutral because it implies a unilateral process of discovering which, on one hand shows the nice

[66] H.-J. Rehm, G. Reed, A. Puhler, P. Stadler, *Biotechnology, Legal, Economical and Ethical Dimensions, Second Completely Revised Edition*, p. 324.

face of a better life and, on other, reveals the irresponsibility of a "progress" without limits and precautions. This is the reason why we can state that all biotechnological controversies also imply bioethical issues.

## I.4. The Tuskegee Syphilis Experiment

In Pence's illustrative book on medical ethics we can read the following paragraph:

> The Tuskegee study of untreated syphilis in hundreds of poor African-American men is one of the most condemned experiments in American medicine. A true understanding of the issues involved requires some historical perspective; but because the study was investigated behind closed doors, its details never became widely known, and it is usually discussed in only simplistic, emotional terms.[67]

This study can be considered as one of the most determinant milestones in the emergence of bioethics since it implied several systematic violations of basic ethical principles and it also tacitly involved the consideration of diverse classes of human beings by denying and neglecting the dignity and most elemental rights of some of them by virtue of their racial, economical and social

---

[67] Pence, Gregory E., *Classic Cases in Medical Ethics*, New York, Mc Graw Hill, 2004, p. 270.

condition. Evidently, the members of National Commission and later Beauchamp and Childress in their seminal book *Principles of Biomedical Ethics* took into consideration this case, among others, to conceive their vision of bioethics, its main goals, tasks and theoretical guidelines. For this reason, it is important that readers know, even if in a synoptic way, what actually happened. The facts were, more or less, as follows.

In 1932, before penicillin was fully developed, treatments for syphilis were both very ineffective and also dangerous because of its toxicity. At that time, there were no scientific parameters to accurately determine whether the possible benefits of the treatments could justify the risks associated with them. Thus, it was impossible to recognize the natural history of the disease, and science lacked relevant information to develop appropriate therapies. It was thought that the solution to the problem was in knowing the natural progression of syphilis; that is, to know what would happen to people infected with it, from the initial stages to the fatal end.

Thus, that same year the American Public Health Service began a clinical investigation that would extend for 40 years, and would become know worlwide as "The Tuskegee Syphilis Experiment." The purposes of the study seemed plausible. However, the procedure chosen to implement it was very controversial, and it has since become the subject of many moral sanctions. The experiment was to study the spontaneous evolution of syphilis in 399 African American subjects, inhabitants of the town of Tuskegee, Maicon County, Alabama, who were apparently duped by scientists into believing that they only had "bad blood" and should be treated sooner.[68] Most of these subjects had a latent syphilis, namely, a secondary syphilis. Therefore, most of them were in the early latent stage. These 399 subjects were never divided into "treatment" or "no treatment" groups. They were all there simply to be studied. Aditionally, a control group was comprised of 201 disease-free individuals. These subjects were observed until 1936, probably due to lack of funds or perhaps because researchers were by then only interested in the "bad blood" group.

It is important to stress that the Tuskegee experiment was not a scientific research properly. There was an evident lack of scientific method while the experiment was carried out:

> There was no central supervision: there were no written protocols; no physician was in charge. Names of the subjects in the study group of 399 were often mixed up with the "controls." The subjects were not housed at any one location or facility.[69]

There were several notorious gaps and inconsistencies in the experiment. Physicians returned only after few years the study had started. Visits were not always documented. There was a hiatus between 1939 and 1948 where no protocols were extended, and no visits were documented. Moreover, between 1963 and 1970 there

[68] For a complete and documented study on this point, see: Jones, James H., *Bad Blood. The Tuskegee Syphilis Experiment*, New and Expanded Edition, New York, The Free Press, 1993.

[69] Pence, Gregory E., *Classic Cases in Medical Ethics*, New York, Mc Graw Hill, 2004, p. 281.

was not any visit to the experimental subjects either. Except the nurse, Eunice Rivers, nobody remained with the subjects. The experiment was quite irregular and was carried out with very sloppy procedures:

> The physicians wanted to know, first, if they had a subject in the study group; and second, if so, how far his syphilis had progressed. To determine the progress of the disease, spinal punctures (called *taps*) were given to 271 of the 399 syphilitic subjects. In spinal tap, a 10-inch needle is inserted between two vertebrae into the cerevrspinal fluid and a small amount of fluid is withdraw – a delicate and uncomfortable process. The subjects were warned to lie very still, lest the needle swerve and puncture the fluid sac, causing infection and other complications.[70]

The reasons for these inconsistences were the absolute irresponsibility and scientific blindness of the physicians in charge, and the total obscurity of the experiment's purposes. In this scientific "initiative," the American Public Health Service got help from the Tuskegee Institute and together started calling for subjects. The opening paragraph said:

> Some time ago you were given a thorough examination and since that time we hope you have gotten a great deal of treatment for bad blood. You will now be given

---

[70] Ibid., pp. 281-82.

> your last chance to get a second examination. This examination is a very special one and after it is finished you will be given a special treatment if it is believed you are in a condition to stand it.[71]

Everyone who wanted to be attended just had to meet a nurse at a specific place, date and hour in order to be transported "to the Tuskegee Hospital for the free treatment."[72] The letter did not alert about any perils and risks for the subjects' health and stressed the study was free of charge. Indeed, the letter finished as follows: "REMEMBER THIS IS YOUR LAST CHANCE FOR SPECIAL FREE TREATMENT. BE SURE TO MEET THE NURSE." It was signed, "Maicon County Health Department."[73]

The letter produced the expected results and the experiment started being carried out. It lasted for 40 years, and even after penicillin was determined to be an effective treatment for syphilis in 1943 the experiment continued without any modifications.

In July 26 of 1972, an investigative report written by Jean Heller of the Associated Press uncovered the experiment and caused its termination:

> For forty years the United States Public health Service (PHS) had been conducting a study of the effects of untreated syphilis on black men in Macon County, Alabama, in an around the country seat of Tuskegee.

---

[71] Undated letter, appended to Dr. Raymond A. Vonderlehr to Dr. Taliaferro Clark, April 21, 1933. National Archives, Washington National Record Center, Suitland, Maryland.
[72] Ibid.
[73] Ibid.

> The Tuskegee Study, as the experiment had come to be called, involved a substantial number of men: 399 who had syphilis and an additional 201 who were free of the disease chosen to serve as controls.[74]

By then, 28 of the 399 subjects had died of syphilis, and an additional 100 had died of various complications as a result of not treating the disease. Furthermore, 19 children contracted syphilis during their period of gestation.[75]

The ethical issues that this study involved were relevant and determined the necessity for the emergence of new deliberative criteria to address moral problems arisen in the medical and scientific fields. Indeed, the Tuskegee Study or, rather, those who conducted it, never considered important issues such as dignity, freedom of choice, harm to subjects, discrimination, and vulnerability, among others. Subjects neither were told about the real purposes of the study nor its possible side effects. Also, they never knew that they had syphilis and the actual severity of the disease. Nobody cared of them, nobody told the truth, and nobody stoped the study. They just were observed. And they just were selected because of their poverty, ignorance, naivete, and color.

[74] *New York Times*, July 26, 1972, pp. 1, 8.

[75] Jones, James H., *Bad Blood. The Tuskegee Syphilis Experiment*, New and Expanded Edition, New York, The Free Press, 1993., p.2.

## I.5. Van Renssealer Potter's Global Bioethics

In 1970, the American oncologist and scholar at the University of Wisconsin, Van Rensselaer Potter published his article "Bioethics, The Science of Survival."[76] In this paper, Potter proposes the name bioethics to define a new discipline which would be able to provide a new wisdom in order for human beings to acquire the "knowledge of how to use knowledge."[77] According to Potter this new wisdom might also be called a "science of survival" since one of the main goals of bioethics must be to improve the quality of life as a whole by promoting the convergence between social sciences and the humanities. In this sense, Potter says that the term bioethics emphasizes "the two most important ingredients in achieving the new wisdom [...]: biological knowdlege and human values".[78]
As Potter conceived of bioethics as a bridge between sciences and humanities, the task of this new discipline must be broad:

> What is needed is a new discipline to provide models of life styles for people who can communicate with each other and propose and explain the new public policies that could provide a "bridge to the future.' The new disciplines will be forged in the heat of today's crisis problems, all of which require some kind of a

[76] *Perspect. Biol. Med.* 14 (1), 1970, pp. 127-153.
[77] Van Renssealer Potter, *Bioethics. Bridge to the Future*, New Jersey, Prentice-Hall, 1971, p. 1.
[78] Ibid. p. 2.

> mix between basic biology, social sciences, and the humanities.[79]

The large scope of bioethics esentially implied its interdisciplinarity, by defining interdisciplinarity as the convergence between sciences and humanities. However, and despite Potter's conception of bioethics as a complementation between ethics and biology, this new discipline should not be considered as a mere mixture of them both:

> Bioethics should examine the nature of human knowledge and its limitations because, in my opinion, it is in this área that the only valid residue of vitalism makes its stand. Bioethics should develop a realistic understanding of biological knowledge and its limitations in order to make recommendations in the field of public policy.[80]

But, what does "a realistic understanding of biological knowledge" mean? Potter neither suggested to abandon traditional science nor to irrationally embrace a new idea. He proposed to cross the boundaries between humanistic and scientific disciplines in order to get a broader visión about human problems arisen by virtue of technological development, and to achieve objective consensus "in terms of the future survival of man and imporvement in the quality of life for future generations."[81] In other words, Potter looked for,

---

[79] Ibid.
[80] Ibid. p. 5.
[81] Ibid. p. 6.

through bioethics, better ways to reexamine scientific premises in order to establish adequate conditions of existence, including individual, social and environmental ones. Therefore, Potter's bioethics would attempt to generate wisdom (the knowledge of how to use the knowledge) in order to reach the social good by seeking a realistic knowledge of human biological nature and of the biological world.

In 1971, Potter published his book *Bioethics. Bridge to the Future* where he insisted on bioethics as a new interdisciplinary knowledge:

> The purpose of this book is to contribute to the future of the human species by promoting the formation of a new discipline, the discipline of *Bioethics*. If there are "two cultures" that seem unable to speak to each other – science and the humanities – and if this is part of the reason that the future seems in doubt, then posibly, we might build a "bridge to teh future" by building the discipline of Bioethics as a bridge between the two cultures.[82]

Beyond these considerations, the book is, essentially, a compilation of Potter's articles which had already appeared in other journals. They did not refer directly to bioethics, with the exception of two of them: the first one "Bioethics a Science of Survival" already quoted, and the last one "Survival as a Goal for Wisdom" where Potter proposes his Bioethical creed.

---

[82] Ibid. p. vii.

Nevertheless, and despite the fact that Potter never specifically defined in his book what bioethics is and what its procedures are, we can find some interesting theoretical milestones which were very important for the subsequent development of the discipline: 1) The concept of dangerous knowledge, 2) Human progress and human survival, 3) The obligation to the future, 4) The control of technology, and 5) The need for an interdisciplinary effort to address the new moral problems arisen in the medical and scientific fields. Potter considered all these issues to redact his bioethical creed which was written as a set of moral imperatives with its respective diagnostics and obligations. As Potter's bioethical creed means the first attemp for establishing a kind of principles of bioethics, I have decide to transcribe them *in extenso*:

1. Belief: *I accept the need for prompt remedial action in a world beset with crises.*
   Commitment: I will work with others to improve the formulation of my beliefs, to evolve additional credos, and to unite in a worldwide movement that will make posible the survival and improved development of the human species in harmony with the natural environment.
2. Belief: *I accept the fact that the future survival and development of mankind, both culturally and biologically, is strongly conditioned by man's present activities and plans.*
   Commitment: I will try to live my own life and to influence the lives of others so as to promote the evolution of a better world

for future generations of mankind, and I will try to avoid actions that would jeopardize their future.

3. Belief: *I accept the uniqueness of each individual and his instinctive need to contribute to the betterment of some larger unit of society in a way that is compatible with the long-range needs of society.*
   Commitment: I will try to listen to the reasoned viewpoint of others whether from a minority or a majority, and I will recognize the role of emotional commitment in producing effective action.
4. Belief: *I accept the inevitability of some human suffering that must result from the natural disorder in biological creatures and in the physical world, but I do not passively accept the suffering that results from man's inhumanity to man.*
   Commitment: I will try to face my own problems with dignity and courage. I will try to assist my fellow men when they are afflicted, and I will work toward the goal of eliminating needless suffering among mankind as a whole.
5. Belief: *I accept the finality of death as a necessary part of life. I affirm my veneration for life, my belief in the brotherhood of man, and my belief that I have an obligation to the future generations of man.*
   Commitment: I will try t olive in a way that will benefit the lives of my fellow men now and in time to come and be remembered favorably by those who survive me.[83]

[83] Ibid. p. 196.

This bioethical creed was conceived as a kind of universal declaration of principles in order to achieve peace, social agreements and conservation of natural resources. Thereby, the main task of bioethics was, according Potter, to improve the quality of life for all human species. Statements of creed did not express absolute and eternal imperatives. Potter did know that the whole world was threatened and influenced by very new events, and he also knew the change in outlook was needed. However, he did not know whether this change would come in time. For this reason, Potter did not consider the statements of the creed as finished products but as principles under "continual reexamination and refinement."[84] Certainly, the global conception of Potter's bioethics meant an important impulse in the transformation of this name into a discipline.

## I.6. André Hellegers

Born in Venlo, Netherlands, he immigrated to the US at the age of 27. He studied medicine in Edinburgh, University of Paris (where he studied Aviation Medicine), Yale University and John Hopkins University (where he did most of his medical research), and as a medic, he specialized in Gynecology and Obstetrics, by becoming a distinguished investigator of the physiology of Fetuses.
Hellegers′ story begins with a troubled childhood, which, according to author Warren Thomas Reich, would shape his view of ethics,

[84] Ibid. p. 194.

medicine, physiology and above all, humans, for his whole life.[85] When Hellegers was born, his parents, scared of having more health impaired sons (Hellegers had a mentally retarded brother), actually believed he was still-born. His father, a banker, approached his baby and poked it with his smoking pipe until, for his great relief, the baby started to cry.[86] Soon, after a year of life, he was thrown down the stairs, resulting with a painful broken back injury which would follow him for the rest of his life, never completely recovering from it. At the age of 23 he was diagnosed with pneumonia and was told that he had only three years left to live.

All these facts shaped his concerns for human health, for human quality of life, and turned him into a philanthropist, always worrying about those in needs. Moreover, the financial disaster that attacked his family early on his childhood made them lose their enormous house and forced them move into a simple house in a small town near Belgium.[87] This would forever remain in Hellegers' mind, and would explain his humble attitude towards money and luxuries. As if that was not enough, his family had to flee the Netherlands all the way to England because of the Second World War.[88] This terrible and traumatic experience of leaving his life behind and witnessing the atrocious state which war brings to existence shaped Hellegers'

---

[85] Reich, Warren T., "The "Wider View": Andre Hellegers's Passionate, Integrating Intellect and the Creation of Bioethics," *Kennedy Institute of Ethics Journal*, Volume 9, Number 1, March 1999, p. 26.

[86] Charlotte Hellegers, Kennedy Institute Twenty-fifth Anniversary Speech, March 12$^{th}$ 1996 (as cited by Warren T. Reich).

[87] Reich, Warren T., "The "Wider View": Andre Hellegers's Passionate, Integrating Intellect and the Creation of Bioethics," *Kennedy Institute of Ethics Journal*, Volume 9, Number 1, March 1999, p. 30.

[88] Ibid. p. 33.

thoughts on the precariousness of human life, furthering even more his concerns for humanity and the needy.

Hellegers had great religious and intellectual influence from his two priest-uncles who are credited for giving him his extraordinary view of life, the "wider view."[89] Both of his uncles were pioneers in creating an integrated world; Uncle Charles was one of the first European worker-priests, his other uncle, André (after whom he was named), founded two missionary orders in China.[90] Thus, he grew up with a religious yet integral view of life.

All of this background information is useful to comprehend and relate to Hellegers' work as a prominent intellectual figure. His fragile childhood and his concerns for life made him take interest in fetuses and early life stages. This would explain his research in those areas and also his special interest in Fertility Control which affected millions of peoples, especially those who were materially impoverished. As the religious man that he was, and being concerned with the debate over fertility that a huge aspect of the Catholic Church doctrine, he participated prominently with other theologians in the discussions. This debate catapulted Hellegers and other prominent intellectual figures such as Daniel Callahan into fame. André Hellegers participated in the "Papal Birth Control Commission" (1964-1966) and President Johnson's Committee on Population and Family Planning (1968-1973). These positions gave him "the possibility to work publicly and effectively at the laying

[89] Ibid. p. 34.
[90] Ibid. p. 35.

open of church and civil society as forums for moral instruction and policy makers" by earning notoriety in the academic world.[91]

At the time he was working at John Hopkins University he also joined the Carroll House, which served as a community where scholars would "engage in the pursuit of truth," and peculiarly, Catholic truth, both revealed and natural; truth in its fullness as theological, metaphysical, scientific and aesthetic."[92] It was in this house where Hellegers formed a group of discussion that academics and theologians of the University would meet to discuss problems of faith and ethics. These discussions soon grabbed the attention of the public, which would gradually start participating more and more. These sessions were thought provoking and helped participants who faced work-related doctrinal problems in their clinical work. They also served as "eye-openers" for the participating clergy, since this discussion approach was more inclusive, with different disciplines participating in ethical debates; moral problems were not dealt with in the "traditional manualistic fashion."[93]

Due to the success of the group, André Hellegers, Father Gouch and archbishop Sheridan came to the conclusion that ethical research on problems about fertility control should be done. Hellegers applied to the Kennedy Foundation and received $50,000 for the foundation of the "Cardinal Gibbons Center at Carroll House." This Center had two main missions: Carry out ethical research on the control of

[91] Ibid. p. 38.

[92] Harvey, John Collins, "Andre Hellegers and Carroll House: Architect and Blueprint for the Kennedy Institute of Ethics," *Kennedy Institute of Ethics Journal*, Volume 14, Number 2, June 2004, p. 202.

[93] Ibid. p. 203.

human fertility and to establish fertility clinics in Catholic Hospitals. This would then turn out to be an important step in Hellegers life, for it would settle the foundations of a bright future.

In the year 1967, Hellegers followed a fellow Hopkins Obstetrician in moving to Georgetown University. His background in participating in the Caroll House discussions gave Hellegers a very insightful perspective on how an academic center for research should work. He had already been successful in combining different disciplines into one comprehensive dialogue about ethical issues arising from the practice of medicine and its implications. Thereby, he would, with the support of his friend Dr. Burns, Father Robert Henle S.J. (who was then the president of Georgetown University), and the Kennedy Foundation led by Eunice Kennedy Shriver and assisted by her husband Sargent Shriver, implement the ideas he had formulated at Caroll House by establishing Georgetown´s Kennedy Institute for the Study of Human Reproduction and Bioethics, at which he would be appointed as founding director. The ideas in André Hellegers' mind about complementation between disciplines, active dialogue, rational discussion and an over-all holistic approach to human knowledge were part of the basis on which the discipline of bioethics was founded some years later.

Probably, Potter`s vision of Bioethics did not rise above Hellegers'. There was a better world-wide reception of Hellegers' bioethical conception due to the formulation Potter gave to his own. Potter thought of bioethics as the "search for wisdom."[94] In contrast, the Georgetown model set by Hellegers` more pragmatic approach

---

[94] Ibid.

should “resolve concrete moral problems.”[95] Also, moral issues tackled by Potter were related to environmental concerns, his bioethical approach had a predominant environmental component, whilst Hellegers’ approach would focus on issues that were of political weight at the time, abuse of the rights of patients, depersonalized medical care, not being allowed to die, all of which are related to the civil rights mentality of the 60’s and 70’s.[96] This, of course, does not mean that Potter had no impact whatsoever in the birth of the discipline, but to what extent and precisely in which areas is not clear at all, after all, some of the Potter’s ideas had intimate relation to those of Hellegers’.[97] Author Thomas Warren Reich notices that both had a global approach to what they considered bioethics should be: “a broad and expansive vision of perspectives, values, concepts and disciplines.”[98]

---

[95] Ibid.
[96] Ibdi. p. 22.
[97] Ibid. p. 24.
[98] Ibid.

# II. FOUNDATIONS

## II.1. The Belmont Report

The Tuskegee case, along with other unethical research (such as that conducted from 1963-1966 on mentally handicapped children in Willowbrook, New York) caused individuals to evaluate techno-scientific progress and the need to morally regulate the experiments resulting from such progress.[99] In the Belmont Report we find the following reflection:

> Scientific research has produced substantial social benefits. It has also posed some troubling ethical questions. Public attention was drawn to these questions by reported abuses of human subjects in biomedical experiments, especially during the Second World War. During the Nuremberg War Crime Trials, the Nuremberg Code was drafted as a set of standards for judging physicians and scientist who had conducted biomedical experiments on concentration camp

[99] The experiment consisted of inoculating the virus of Hepatitis to healthy children in order to study the effects of gamma globulin as a possible treatment.

> prisoners. This code became the prototype of many later codes intended to assure that research involving human subjects would be carried out in an ethical manner.[100]

The Belmont Report was the result of four years of work by the National Commission for the Protection of Human Subjects of Biomedical and Behavioral Research, created by the Congress of the United States of America in 1974 with the following aims: i) to discuss and reflect about the limits of techno-scientific research, ii) to evaluate the balance between the risks and benefits of the human research, iii) to provide guidelines for an equitable selection of human subjects participating in such experiments, and iv) to think about the nature, scope and meaning of Informed Consent in scientific research.[101]

Thus, the National Comission's general aim was to create a deliberative framework for complex problems inherent in scientific experimentation. In this regard, the Belmont Report identifies as its primary purpose:

> Identify the basic ethical principles that should underlie the conduct of biomedical and behavioral research involving human subjects and to develop guidelines

[100] National Commission for the Protection of Human Subjects of Biomedical and Behavioral Research, *Belmont Report. Ethical Principles and Guidelines for the Protection of Human Subjects of Research,* US Government Printing Office, Reprint from the collection of the University of Michigan Library, 2009, Appendix Volume I, 78-0012.
[101] Ibdi., Appendix Volume II, 78-0014.

> which should be followed to assure that such research is conducted in accordance with those principles.[102]

The Belmont Report gathered and summarized all the results of the National Commission's work, defining three fundamental principles that the Commission had identified as absolutely necessary to protect human subjects of experimentation. The idea was, first, to eliminate excessive paternalism from scientific practice and medicine, which traditionally had not considered the opinions of the subjects and patients as an important element in the implementation of research and treatment. Thus, it attempted give prominence to individual autonomy by allowing human subjects to participate in the deliberation and decision about procedures and treatments that could be applied to them.

Secondly, it attempted to restore the respect for human dignity trying to maximize the benefits for patients and subjects, and reduce the risks that could cause them harm or injury.

And third, the Belmont Report showed the need for equal treatment of patients and human experimentation subjects, giving them equal rights in various important stages of research and treatment. Here we might highlight the following: 1. Fair methods for choosing them, 2. Fair distribution of efforts to safeguard the dignity, health and life of those involved, and 3. Avoidance of any type of discrimination in human subjects research and in medical treatment of people, whatever their origin, race or status.

[102] Ibid., Appendix Volume I, 78-0012.

We can understand, then, the Belmont Report as the first formulation of bioethical principles. These principles have since enjoyed a rapid and growing acceptance, extending to the field of medical care where they regulate the most important aspects of the doctor-patient relationship. However, the principles were, according to the same National Commission, general guidelines whose primary purpose was to assist in the deliberation of particularly complex cases, guiding decision-making and moral reasoning by providing criteria for choosing the correct courses of action to be followed in each case. Moreover, the National Commission also claimed that the principles were a sufficiently solid theoretical framework from which individuals could generate more specific rules that would finally create procedures that could be applied on a practical level.[103]

Thus, the Belmont Report emphasized the importance of distinguishing clearly between the nature of research, its limits, scope and possible implications for the lives and safety of human subjects. The report was structured in three parts in which the principles are discussed, highlighting various aspects of their implementation: A. Boundaries between Practice and Research, B. Basic Ethical Principles, and C. Applications. I will discuss each one of them briefly and separately.[104]

---

[103] "These principles cannot always be applied so as to resolve beyond dispute particular ethical problems. The objective is to provide an analytical framework that will guide the resolution of ethical problems arising from research involving human subjects". *The Belmont Report*, p. 3.

[104] Moreover, The Belmont Report has an extensive Appendix, divided into two volumes, containing the full text of the papers that were prepared to assist the National Comission in

*A. Boundaries between Practice and Research*

In this part, the Report stressed the necessity of distinguishing between biomedical behavioral research and therapeutic treatment. The fundamental objective of this distinction was to determine which activities should be thoroughly reviewed to protect human subjects of experimentation. Moreover, this part emphasized the distinction between practice and research, indicating that the first one is an intervention to emphasize the welfare of the patient, giving him proper diagnosis and treatment, and the second is an activity whose purpose is to test a hypothesis, reach conclusions and develop or contribute to a general moral knowledge on biomedical research. The Report emphasizes that both purposes needed to take into account respect for the dignity, integrity and well-being of the individuals involved and have a high degree of scientific conviction in regard to the safety and effectiveness of therapy.

*B. Basical Ehical Principles*

As I have already indicated, the expression "Basic Ethical Principles" in the Belmont Report refers to the main moral milestones in our Western cultural tradition. The specific aim of The National Commission was to identify the most universally accepted principles of our moral tradition and determine which best suited the moral demands of research involving human subjects. The principles were as follows:

---

its work and its consideration of the basic ethical principles that should underlie the conduct of research involving human subjects.

1. *Respect for Persons*: This principle recognizes persons as free agents and worthy of protection in the event that their autonomy is diminished or absent. It represents, on the one hand, an individual right that is related to the ability of each individual to make decisions and act upon them, and secondly, it implies the duty to respect that autonomy. Moreover, this principle involves the explicit recognition of individual freedom and the capacity for self-determination inherent in every human being. Where this faculty is notoriously reduced, the patient has the right to be represented in his decisions.

We will see later how the dichotomy between, on one hand, rights and duties, and on other, between individual autonomy and paternalism, are a major problem for bioethical principlism, especially when determining whether a principle points to an inalienable individual right or a binding and universal duty associated with the supposed objectivity of scientific and medical paternalism. Furthermore, it is important to consider the possible contradictions that might occur between the individual will of research subjects and the duty to protect them.

2. *Beneficence*: The Report is emphatic in noting that this principle should be understood beyond traditional kindness or charity. Rather, it is a moral obligation to promote the wellbeing of an individual at every stage of the investigation and to avoid injuring him by all means possible. In this sense, the document formulated "two general rules as complementary expressions of beneficent actions: (1) do no harm and (2) maximize possible benefits and minimize possible

harms."[105] Although this principle is based on the Hippocratic Oath, the members of the National Commission showed flexibility in its scope with respect to beneficence. Their reformulation of the oath clearly has utilitarian roots, which poses a major problem for this principle. Hippocrates conceived the principle of "do no harm" deontologically; namely, as an absolute obligation that must be respected even at the expense of the greater overall good. In other words, the Hippocratic Oath implies never hurt a person even if such damage could mean greater benefits to other individuals. However, The National Commission discusses this definition leaving a potential latent dilemma:

> Further, the Hippocratic Oath requires physicians to benefit their patients "according to their best judgment." Learning what will in fact benefit may require exposing persons to risk. The problem posed by these imperatives is to decide when it is justifiable to seek certain benefits despite the risks involved, and when the benefits should be foregone because of the risks.[106]

Thus, the principle of beneficence which is closely linked to the principle of respect for persons can be tragically separated from the latter. This generates an intractable antinomy for bioethics. The

---

[105] National Commission for the Protection of Human Subjects of Biomedical and Behavioral Research, *Belmont Report. Ethical Principles and Guidelines for the Protection of Human Subjects of Research*, US Government Printing Office, Reprint from the collection of the University of Michigan Library, 2009, Appendix Volume I, 78-0012.
[106] Ibid., p. 5.

Report understands autonomy in a paternalistic way. This means whoever ultimately determines what is good for the patient is who oversees the treatment and research. However, there are times when that conception does not match the subject or patient, generating an almost unbridgeable gap when the principle is applied as a deliberative criterion to scientific practice. In other words, this principle works properly only when both the patient and the agent have the same concept of what "the beneficial" for the former is. Otherwise, beneficence can covertly become a principle which, in practice, does not respect individual autonomy and is unilaterally imposed.

3. *Justice*: This principle points to the duty of equitably distributing benefits of research among involved subjects and to avoid risks to the most vulnerable groups. It also seeks to ensure that the selection of research subjects is carried out without any kind of discrimination as occurred in such cases as Tuskegee, Willowbrook and the Nazi Death Camps during the Second World War. It is thus a principle of distributive justice from which the members of the National Commission asked themselves important questions, such as who determines what "to be equal" means, or what the criterion should be set for defining what "fair treatment". In this regard, the Report recognized five criteria: (1) to each person an equal share, (2) to each person according to individual need, (3) to each person according to individual effort, (4) to each person according to societal contribution, and (5) to each person according to merit.[107] The problem is that each formulation excludes the others, and it is

[107] Ibid., p. 6.

unclear what should be imposed over the other if in the deliberation is present more than one. I will discuss this problem later.

*C. Applications*

In this part, the Report identifies three fundamental requirements for implementing the principles described above. These requirements represent, at least in theory, actual conditions of possibility, and are adjusted, each one of them, at a specific principle.

1. *Informed Consent* (requirement for application of the principle of Respect for Persons): It considers three elements as conditions of its accomplishment:

*Information*: The person must be fully informed about posible risks associated with the investigation or the procedure. This information must be given in a timely manner and should include, among other things, the research procedure, its purposes and any risks associated with experimentation.

*Comprehension*: Information must be given so that the individual fully understands the nature and extent of the procedure. Taking into account that intelligence, rationality, maturity and language are different among people, it will be necessary to adapt the process of presenting information according to the subject´s capacities.

*Voluntariness*: Consent is valid if it is informed but also voluntary. This means that every human subject must express his acceptance (agreement) to engage in some experimentation without any coercion or undue influence. This requirement means we must make the difficult distinction between justifiable persuasion and undue influence, which certainly is a very hard task if we try to analyze this issue from a completely objective perspective.

Another aspect that deserves further consideration and clarity is the problem with the application of Informed Consent procedure. We know that this is the conscious, competent and fully informed acceptance of a procedure or therapy by a human subject. However, we will see that when we bring the procedure into practice, its definition has some problems. We can analyze these problems from several questions.

Is it the central objective of Informed Consent to allow subjects or patients to participate in medical decisions? If Informed Consent involves recognizing the autonomy of the person concerned, is it its purpose to allow that person to make the decision? Is the research subject or patient co-responsible for the consequences arising from the application of a particular procedure or treatment? Is it the purpose of Informed Consent to protect the scientist or researcher against the legal responsibility for any harmful consequence that affects a particular subject? Is Informed Consent just looking for a procedure in order to help people understand what a treatment means, but not finally decides for themselves? Will the autonomy of the concerned person be respected only if it matches the scientist's or physician's will? If the patient or human research subject has not given his consent, should we always respect his decision, regardless of the consequences that this decision involves? Is Informed Consent definitely binding? If an individual is unable to decide for himself, when can we be reasonably sure that the will of his representatives matches the individual's?

All these questions, which I will leave unanswered for the moment, demonstrate that the concept of autonomy is still understood in a very conditioned and restricted way within bioethics. I will come back later to this particular problem.

2. *Assessment of Risks and Benefits* (requirement for application of the principle of Beneficence): it implies we ought to determine the nature and scope of the risks and benefits with the systematic assessment of each. This protocol will help the researcher to determine whether the proposed research is properly designed. For the review committee it will be a method for clarifying whether the risks are justified, and it will represent a means for the subjects decide whether to participate in research or refuse to do it.

3. *Selection of Subjects* (requirement for application of the principle of Justice): it implies the existence of fair procedures and outcomes in the selection of research subjects. This selection has two levels on which justice can be applied: individual and societal. Individual justice implies the fairness of the researchers; namely, "they should not offer potentially beneficial research only to some patients" with special features or select only "undesirable" subjects for risky experimentation. Social justice means the distinction between classes of subjects that ought, or ought not, participate in any kind of research, should be based on their ability to bear burdens and "on the appropriateness of placing further burdens on already burdened persons".[108]

[108] Ibid., p. 11.

## II.2. Philosophical Foundations of Principlism

The principles of the Belmont Report are closely related to the principles of Biomedical Ethics of Beauchamp and Childress. We may consider the latter as a substantial expansion and redefinition of the former. However, it would be a mistake to say that The Belmont Report provided an abstract framework for the Beauchamp and Childress' book. In other words, The Belmont Report was not the starting point of *The Principles of Biomedical Ethics,* they were simultaneous works. Tom Beauchamp has said about it:

> They have wrongly assumed that *Belmont* preceded and grounded *Principles*. The two Works were written simultaneously, the one inevitably influencing the other. There was reciprocity in the drafting, and influence ran bilaterally. I was often simultaneously drafting material on the same principle or topic both for the National Comission and for my colleague Childress, while he was at the same time writing material for me to inspect. I would routinely write parts of the *Belmont Report* during the day at the National Comission headquarters on Westbard Avenue in Bethesda, then go to my office at Georgetown in the evening and draft parts of chapters for Childress to review. Despite their entirely independent origins, these projects grew up and matured together[109].

[109] Beauchamp, Tom, "The Origins and Evolution of *The Belmont Report*", in Childress, J., Meslin, Eric M. and Shapiro, Harold T. (Editors), *Belmont Revisited. Ethical Principles for Research with Human Subjects*, Georgetown University Press, 2005, p. 15.

However, the work and conclusions of these authors are clearly inspired by diverse milestones in the history of Western ethics. While in the formulation of principles, Beauchamp and Childress recognize strong influence of recent ethical authors, such as Ross and Frankena, it is also possible to verify that the basis of their approach was influenced by the ideas of classical thinkers such as Aristotle, Hume Kant and Mill. In the following section, I will briefly describe the main topics of those authors that are present in the *The Principles of Biomedical Ethics*.

*Aristotle*

In *The Principles of Biomedical Ethics* we can find several Aristotelian concepts, such as freedom, autonomy and good. However, I think the main relationships between Aristotle and *The Principles* is built from the concept of virtue which is tacitly present in the formulation of the main ideas of Beauchamp and Childress related to the principles of Beneficence and Nonmaleficence.

Aristotle defines moral action as that which leads people to the full realization of their potential being; that is, every action which, according to a criterion of virtue, impels man to achieve an end "given by nature - which is Happiness. In this connection, Aristotle affirms "the virtue of man also will be the state of character which makes a man good and which makes him do his own work well".[110] Thus, virtue is not an external power of things or a mere passion or faculty. Virtue is a way of being, a state of character, in the sense of

[110] Aristotle, *Nicomachean Ethics*, in McKeon, Richard (Ed.), *The Basic Works of Aristotle*, New York, The Modern Library, 2001, p. 957, II 6 1106a 22-24.

revealing the *internal and natural* will of something toward the good. Moreover, Aristotle defines virtue as the means between two vices, one by excess and another one by default. In other words, virtue is “the mean relative to us, this being determined by a rational principle, and by that principle by which the man of practical wisdom would determine it”.[111]

But, how can we recognize the means? In Book VI of his *Ethics*, Aristotle stresses that there is a special virtue that can help us to do it: practical wisdom (*phronesis*). He who possesses this virtue also has the ability to perform well and correctly. In other words, that person has the ability to know what to do in order to resolve complex situations and how to deliberate on a moral dilemma. However, this kind of virtue is not only acquired by practice but by intellectual learning. Deliberation needs time and preparation, it does not bloom automatically. Only that individual who is wise in the practice, who knows how to deliberate and make decisions will be able to recognize the right means, namely the other virtues. “The man who is capable of deliberating has practical wisdom”.[112] This reveals a close and interesting relationship between Aristotelian ethics and *The Principles*. Diverse concepts, such as excellence, perfection, practical wisdom (*prudence*), justice, fairness and virtue, are important benchmarks for the bioethicist and they could guide right decisión makings. In other words, virtue allows proper

[111] Ibid., p. 959, II 6 1107a 37-39.
[112] Ibid., p. 1026, VI 5 1140a 31-32.

deliberation and the application of plausible and reasonable procedures in both the medical and scientific fields.[113]

Finally, Aristotelian ethics provides another important element for bioethics. In the Modern Age Ethics had been confined to a subjective realm, and the effort of enlightened philosophers to give it a scientific and rational character was in vain. Because of that, the contemporary man - as an individual and as a social and political entity - is called to retrieve the status of rationality for philosophical ethics. This effort demonstrates the currentness of Aristotelian ethics since it poses a different concept of practical rationality, beyond the formal or intellectualist. This practical Ethics is perhaps the only one able to carry out, with some success, the task and challenge to reflect on bases and procedures for dealing with complex moral dilemmas caused by the excessive techno-scientific power of the current era.

*Hume*

Hume's ethics is based on the assumption that men have a natural interest in sustaining society. Thus, man can only manage contradictions in matters of morality by living in society. In *An Inquiry Concerning the Principles of Morals*, Hume defines morality as a phenomenon that must be explained in terms of human nature. This philosopher affirms that passions motivate action and the reason is subordinate to them. Human passions are motivated by pleasure and displeasure and the unique purpose of moral judgments

[113] Aristotle himself emphasizes the special practical feature of his ethics: He says "the present inquiry does not aim at theoretical knowledge like the others (for we are inquiring not in order to know what virtue is, but in order to become good, since otherwise our inquiry would have been of no use)". Ibid., p. 953, II 1103 b 26 – 29.

is to guide action. Therefore, the virtuous action is that which produces pleasure and the vicious one is that which causes displeasure. As human beings share their nature, which determines their feelings, they finally will feel the same as their fellow man and therefore will coincide on moral judgments and the ranking of the vatious virtues.

Hume distinguishes between individual virtues and social virtues. Social virtues are more important, because they somehow allow tolerance and common life in order to obtain the greatest possible utility for society and therefore for each individual. In this way, a society will tend to approve that which causes more utility and to disapprove that which produces more pain and discomfort. Therefore, the public space contains genuine moral feelings, stemming from the principles of utility and benevolence which are universal because human nature is shared by all persons. Virtue is not acting according to right reason but according to a pleasurable action that leads us to approve a particular action and no other. To act according to virtue means to act according the principle of the greater utility for us and for all.

Therefore, acting according to the principle of utility will also mean considering justice as a superior virtue to others, on an equal level with benevolence. In this way, both justice and benevolence are social virtues that are revealed as more useful than the particular virtues, because through them it is possible to achieve social cohesion and peaceful coexistence.

The moral conception of Hume and especially his notion of virtue are well represented in the work of Beauchamp and Childress, especially on the principles of nonmaleficence, beneficence and justice. These ultimately appeal to common human nature which, in some cases, should be able to prioritize particular and immediate good beneath social and perishable good. In addition, Beuchamp and Childress highlight, like Hume, the need to unite the abstract concept of virtue with good practices; namely, reinforce it with eminent skills and qualities that exalt its status as virtue. A famous paragraph of Hume can help to ratify the above:

> It may be esteemed, perhaps, a superflious task to prove, that the benevolent or softer affections are estimable, and wherever they appear, engage the approbation and good-will of mankind. The epithets sociable, good-natured, humane, merciful, grateful, friendly, generous, beneficent, or their equivalents, are known in all languages, and universally express the highest merit, which human nature is capable of attaining. Where these amiable qualities are atended with birth and power and eminent abilities, and display themselves in the good government or useful instruction of mankind, they seem even to raise the poswessors of them above the Rank of human nature, and make them approach in some measure to the divine[114].

[114] Hume, David, *An Enquiry Concerning the Principles of Morals*, USA, Wilder Publications, 2008, p. 9.

*Kant*

Kant proposed that all metaphysics of morals, and especially his own, must transcend the sphere in which the good is aligned to being, and to become a theoretical illustrated nomenclature that speaks in terms of wrong or right.[115] Thus, he seeks to discover a new foundation for ethics, which is not like the Aristotelian metaphysical but with a rational basis; that is, a universal and necessary foundation for all individuals, because reason is the only thing shared by all humans.

Thereby, it would determine the behavior of rational beings by principles of a contingent nature. Their will is the capacity to determine for themselves through the representation of certain laws called imperatives. For Kant, most of the imperatives through which rational beings modulate their activities, actions and moral conduct, are hypothetical. Their realization depends on favorable or unfavorable consequences. For Kant, the foundation of ethics is not into these kinds of imperatives, because subjectivity is the source of many moral foundations. The Kantian ethical imperative must represent itself in universal Law as rational criterion of morality, and it must prescind from contingent and emotive elements. It is an unconditional imperative; namely, a categorical mandate.

Kant states the first formulation of the categorical imperative, as follows: "Act only according to that maxim whereby you can at the

---

[115] For a more thorough review of Kant's Ethics see Ross, David, *Kant's Ethical Theory*, Oxford, 1969. Also, Deleuze, Gilles, *La philosophie critique de Kant*, Paris, Presses Universitaires de France, 1963.

same time will that it should become a universal law."[116] This formulation transforms the imperative in a criterion for discerning the moral actions from which are not moral, according to whether they can (or cannot) be universalized. The maxim or particular principle whereby an individual directs his action must be capable of universalization. A maxim is moral when it can be universal. The correct moral act is one that emanates from the adequacy of our individual maxims and universal Law. Moral action must be thought without self-contradiction, as a universal practice of a particular community. Reason is the foundation of Kantian ethics, and duty is the heart of its structure.

Thus, for Kant, freedom as autonomy of will is the foundation of moral action. A free moral agent is one capable of self-legislation; namely to create for itself its own rules and obey them in terms of the duty involved in that act. Although the Kantian concept of autonomy is not the same as that emphasized by *The Principles of Biomedical Ethics* (which provides significant value to paternalism, limiting individual autonomy), it is important to take it into account because it recognizes the importance of an autonomous subject. This subject is one who is capable of making moral decisions by discovering the right thing through his reason within a moral community, characterized by respect and freedom of individuals.

However, the criterion that Kant offers is, at least, logical and not strictly moral. Its basis is the absence of contradiction. We could not

[116] Kant, Immanuel, *Grounding for the Metaphysics of Morals,* 3rd ed., Hackett. pp. 30: Translate by James W. Ellington. Also see: *Fondements de la métaphysique des moeurs*, Paris, Librairie Delagrave, 1939; Translate by Victor Delbos.

universalize the lying maxim because that would be irrational since, sooner or later, we ourselves would be victims of lies. The act of lying is immoral not because it is bad, wrong or reprehensible, but simply because what it supports is not susceptible to universalization. As Jonas has said, the categorical imperative is not a principle of objective responsibility because the moral consequences of its application never come to be considered: they are only an expression of mind.[117] This undoubtedly represents an important difference between Kantian autonomy and the principle of Respect for Autonomy of Beauchamp and Childress.

*Mill*

The principal reference of modern utilitarianism is John Stuart Mill. Strongly influenced at first by the ideas of Bentham, his philosophy is a reworking of the liberal British empiricist tradition begun by Locke. In his book *A System of Logic, Ratiocinative and Inductive* (1843), Mill argues that empiricism, a philosophy based on experience, optimizes the structure of society, and that the moral cohesion, which is necessary in civil space, arises from the utilitarian ethics. His main contribution to the theory, which leads us away from a purely quantitative possition is his distinction between higher and lower pleasures. Both sides should not be looked at in the same way because they correspond to different declinations of human passion, which do not necessarily lead to happiness, and may be guided by pseudomoral criteria or criteria of a mere bodily

[117] Jonas, Hans, *Das Prinzip Veranwortung: Versuchi einer Ethic für die Tecnologische Zivilisation*, Francfort am Main, Insel Verlag, 1988.

nature. Thus, Mill faces the following objection to Bentham's conception. If the majority of people were accustomed to lower pleasures and considered them desirable, would they necessarily be happy? Maybe not, as society would not be able to sustain itself if the conduct of its citizens was only inspired in the pursuit of passionate happiness:

> It is better to be a human being dissatisfied than a pig satisfied; better to be Socrates dissatisfied than a fool satisfied. And if the fool, or the pig, are of a different opinion, it is because they only know their own side of the question. The other party to the comparison knows both sides.[118]

Thus, Mill moves away from Bentham's conception because he introduces the concept of quality of pleasure as a criterion of moral rightness, against the arithmetic principles that Bentham proposed. How can we know the superiority of one type of pleasure over another? Mill responds as who has experienced both sides of the coin; namely, the pleasures of the body as the spirit can only do it. That individual is a competent tribunal, equally related to both poles and, therefore, is capable to distinguish between the lowest and highest pleasures. Mill rejects the identification of utilitarianism with a "doctrine of swine". Therefore, it would be an error to think pleasures do not differ in degree and kind.

---

[118] Mill, John Stuart, *Utilitarianism*, New York, The Liberal Arts Press, 1948, p. 14.

Beyond the concept of utility, as present in the work of Beauchamp and Childress, the distinction between quality and quantity of pleasure made by Mill is essential in order to understand that it is unreasonable to take any action just because it is evaluated as useful. In fact, if we would have seriously considered this distinction we would have prevented many deaths and many injuries to humans who have been victims of the excessive appetite of contemporary scientific progress.

However, the hedonistic principle of *sacrifice of minorities*, present in the utilitarian theory, seems inconsistent with the moral standards of any civilized society. Is it moral to achieve the greatest happiness of the greatest number of individuals by postponing indefinitely the welfare of those who, because of various reasons, have fallen outside of that majority? Is it possible to show a consistent Ethic with the current conditions of existence, from the maxima of demanding minorities to renounce their identity and tradition, their legitimate aspirations and differences, because they are not in the majority?

*Ross*

Ross believes, as did Kant, that there are obligations that must be respected. Nevertheless, he goes one step further than the German philosopher, by first distinguishing between different types of obligations and, secondly, by noting that there are obligations that must be evaluated according to the particular circumstances. This distinction between obligations has represented a very important element in the construction of the Principlism of Beauchamp and Childress. Let us examine this further.

In his Ethics, Ross distinguishes between *prima facie* obligations and real obligations. The first ones are obligations with a provisional character. However, like the real obligations of a situation, the *prima facie* obligations should be assessed and categorized according to the circumstances and the principles involved in each case. Ross has said:

> Although I think it is quite clear that a promise creates a *prima facie* obligation, or a responsibility, quite different from tha which alone the utilitarian system recognizes, we must guard against stating the obligation in a way which would lead to consequences which our reflective moral consciousness would reject.[119]

Contrary to what might be expected, the ethics of Ross is not a traditional casuistry theory. Within his understanding of the *prima facie* obligations it is possible to recognize certain moral principles which cannot be violated and which generate certain irreducible obligations.

*Prima facie* obligations are those which Ross called obligations of self-perfection, which are directly related to the principles of biomedical ethics of Beauchamp and Childress. These obligations are justice, beneficence and nonmaleficence, which, of course,

---

[119] Ross, W. David, *Foundations of Ethics*, London, Oxford at the Clarendon Press, 1951, p.108.

involve moral principles. However, Ross does not provide criteria for discerning or ranking among the different principles related to these obligations. All that he said, broadly, is that in case of conflict between beneficence and nonmaleficence, the latter should always prevail.

Beyond this fundamental contribution to bioethics, the thought of Ross also emphasizes the fact that one must be very cautious in determining the actual weight of the obligations involved in especially problematic cases. Therefore, the importance of each case must be examined, not only from the level of the circumstances but also in the level of the judgments about the principles involved in the deliberation.

*Frankena*

Frankena gives bioethics an interesting theoretical deepening of the principles of utility and justice. Utility emphasizes the importance of consequences as a criterion of moral correctness, and justice emphasizes the central role that correspond the duties guiding any kind of deliberation. In case of conflict or contradiction between these principles, Frankena points out that justice should be imposed over utility. Thus, both justice and utility are *prima facie* principles and do not represent real duties. This makes the Ethics of Frankena closer to the deontological realm. Nevertheless, it goes one step further: considering the possible consequences as a deliberative criterium.

Frankena's argument does not seem controversial. It is very difficult, perhaps impossible, not to associate a good moral act to the production of a good. In this sense, the consequences are indisputable indicators that the goodness or badness of an action can be measured through them. However, if doing good is only a virtue, not an obligation, it is also undeniable that producing good is, *prima facie*, a good action. Thus, Frankena believes that the principle of justice is derived from the utility. It should be noted here that both principles are part of morality, but not everything fair is good and vice versa.

However, Frankena emphasizes the existence of another principle which is even more important for bioethics: the principle of beneficence, which is related to the duty of prioritizing good over evil. Frankena says:

> We have a prima facie obligation to maximize the balance of good over evil only if we have *a priori* prima facie obligation to do good and prevent harm. I shall call this prior principle the *principle of beneficence*. The reason I call it the principle of *beneficence* and not the principle of *benevolence* is to underline the fact that it asks us actually to do good and not evil, not merely to want or will to do so.[120]

This means that Frankena includes the principle of nonmaleficence of Beauchamp and Childress in his principle of beneficence. This would emphasize the obligation to do good over evil in all circumstances. However, Frankena does not explicit what good and

---

[120] Frankena, William, *Ethics*, Second Edition, New Jersey, Prentice Hall, 1973, p. 45.

evil are and thus this problem persists both in the level of *prima facie* obligations and the level of consequences which are always *a posteriori*.

Beyond these foundations, bioethical principlism implies tacitly other importants contemporary philosophical sources:

*Jonas*

The Jonas's ethics of responsibility holds that the Cartesian paradigm caused the technological objectification of the world and the split between man and nature. Therefore, Jonas understands the history of metaphysics culmination not only as an irreversible expression of technological power. For him it is the foundation of his ethics, because he states that the human being's end is in nature, namely, in the being.

Thereby, the main novelty and contribution of Jonas's ethics is the complementariness between ends and duties as deliberative procedure. The imperative of responsibility is conceived not only as the possibility to impute to human beings the acts that they commit but, above all, as an obligation to limit techno-scientific power, which is able to alter the conditions of life as a whole. Jonas's proposal is consistent with the need for ethics aimed more at public policy than private actions. This important feature of Jonas' ethics has a strong relation to one of the most relevant bioethics' aims: to balance individual autonomy with social justice.

Now, in the ethic of responsibility, teleology and deontology are two different but complementary branches of moral reasoning. Such is the cornerstone of bioethics. The unmasking of this divorce, and its contemporary reception, in the form of a complementation, points to the principle of responsibility. This principle could avoid the theoretical difficulties related to the search for moral correctness criteria that satisfy current existence conditions.

The ethics of responsibility could be seen as a teleological ethic. Its moral correctness criterion proposes a goal to reach, namely, it considers consequences action's responsibility. This ethics distinguishes two stages in the history of technology: the pre-modern technology, related to a "traditional" ethics that Jonas called "ethics given so far," and modern technology, which must be covered from the principle of responsibility[121]. This ethics also combines modernity with the idea of progress. Humanity generates discoveries with a syncopated rhythm. The techno-scientific challenge means to avoid total disaster, and that implies the capability to previse, with a high degree of accuracy, the true consequences of technical action. Nature is unable to reverse damage and devastation caused by relentless technological colonization. This is the sad human action corollary whose scope is, in time and place, beyond all possibility of calculation.

Thereby, and in close harmony with bioethics' goals, Jonas suggests a new foundation for contemporary morality, a new imperative that requires the preservation of an authentic human life and respect for the genetic identity of a species. Thus, the ethic of responsibility could be understood as a caring ethics being, because it only aims to

---

[121] See, Jonas, Hans, *Das Prinzip Veranwortung: Versuchi einer Ethic für die Tecnologische Zivilisation*, Francfort am Main, Insel Verlag, 1988, p. 17 and following.

care for and maintain what already exists, and it does not pretend to improve current living conditions.

> All this has decisively changed. Modern technology has introduced actions of such novel scale, objects and consequences that the framework of former ethics can no longer contain them. The *Antigone* chorus on the *denoites*, the wondrous power, of man would have to read differently now; and its admonition to the individual to honor the laws mof the land would no longer be enough. The goods, too, whose venerable rightcould check the headlong rush of human action, are long gone. To be sure, the old prescriptions of the "neighbor" ethics – of justice, charity, honesty and so on – still hold in their intimate immediacy for the nearest, day-by-day sphere of human interaction. But this sphere is overshadowed by a growing realm of collective action where doer, deed, and effect are no longer the same as they were in the proximate sphere, and which by the enormity of its power forces upon ethics a new dimension of responsibility never dreamed of before.[122]

Thus, there is a tragic antinomy in contemporary culture. On the one hand, we have the technological actions necessity. On the other, the difficulty of finding ethical principles that brought universal validity to moral norms that govern such actions. There would be a

[122] Jonas, Hans, *The Imperative of Responsibility. In Search of an Ethics for the Technological Age*, The University of Chicago Press, 1985, p. 6.

considerable risk to the planet and its inhabitants, from the disproportionate amount of current human technology. This danger would be increased by the little government intervention in the collective responsibility for consequences and implications of technological actions. Thus, moral norms, that govern technological colonization, must be universally recognized and agreed.

Jonas argues that technology has accompanied human beings from their appearance. The use of tools allowed for the satisfaction of human needs. *Homo Faber* precedes *Homo Sapiens* on the evolutionary chain. Making preceded the ability to previse (ability to anticipate). Subsequently, *Homo Sapiens* would have been reaffirmed as an individual capable of doing (making) science and capable of calculating and preventing the consequences of its actions.

However, mankind's ontological status would have regressed. Through its power and technological scope, humanity expresses an enormous power that now includes the ability to genetically manipulate and change life. However, mankind does not have equal capacity to foresee the exact consequences of its actions. It is only able to presuppose them. Technology that was a controllable and finite means has become an unstoppable discovery and conquest momentum which surpasses itself. Thereby, technology, beyond its questionable objectivity, is becoming a dangerous and multifactorial conjunction of subjective ends.[123]

---

[123] Jonas, Hans, *Das Prinzip Veranwortung: Versuchi einer Ethic für die Tecnologische Zivilisation*, Francfort am Main, Insel Verlag, 1988, p. 30.

This development generates, according to Jonas, a dynamic that overpowers the will of man, through a sort of technological challenge that requires the implementation of all that, which, in theory, is seen as possible. This basically means that we are losing control of the technology and thus, we are losing freedom. Technological progress has been consolidated in the current world and it is able to go even against the human will. The source of this dynamic movement is in a close relationship between scientific progress and technological development. Science, for its development, will require increasingly sophisticated instruments and thus transforms technology into a kind of giant laboratory that must make all necessary elements to continue discovering.

Jonas argues that as the ultimate result from this development, nature has become vulnerable to human action. Therefore, there currently exists, a total gap between it and traditional ethical reflection, due to ethics unknown, for reasons already alluded to above, the responsibility towards the environment. The unusual power that contemporary subject has, shows the urgency to find grounds for universally valid rules. However, the difficulty of finding these foundations would come, according to Jonas, from the chasm that contemporary philosophy opened between reality, axiologically neutral, and the knower subject, which would be the only source of value. It will be necessary then to generate an ethic of responsibility, to take charge of that division between being and consciousness.

Jonas proposes to extend the human responsibility, consistent with the expansion of the scope of human action. His new ethics will

consider these issues in its reflection and will complement traditional ethics. Jonas proposes to configure a new imperative, which in one of its formulations says: "Act so that the effects of your action are compatible with the permanence of genuine human life"[124]. Unlike Kant, who appealed to the encapsulated correlation between act and subject, the new imperative implies a wider tuning between the consequences of acts and the survival of human beings.
In opposition to Kant's categorical imperative, which is an imaginary exercise in each particular consciousness, Jonas seeks an objective responsibility principle, related to public policies and to the consequences of acts, because they are relevant for moral reasoning. Thus, while individual actions require only traditional ethics rules, Jonas intends to conform to the current conditions of existence, where human action is modified by techno-scientific progress, and he proposes a more reaching imperative where moral standards are required to submit "a real future as an opened place to our responsibility"[125].
Thus, the proper Kantian moral reckoning, is complemented by the new imperative because it adds a perspective of future that categorical imperative has not. Thereby, the imperative of Jonas overcomes the enlightened and moral subjectivity because it implies a concrete and objective future as the horizon of human responsibility. Thus, Jonas considers the real and concrete consequences of human action and a futuristic factor in responsibility as a moral foundation of universal value. His idea of

[124] Ibid.,p. 32-33.
[125] Ibid., p.33

the future, unlike the utopian, is conceived more as a threat than a harbinger of a promised dawn.

According to Jonas, genuine human life involves two basic elements: first, preservation of environment and biodiversity. Anthropocentrism rooted in "traditional" ethics does not include a concern for the preservation of nature. However, Jonas thinks that nature has its own moral rights which new imperative does not seek to substantiate or explain, but simply takes it as axiom[126].

Jonas' thought involve the assumption that freedom and creative skills, and evaluative abilities, should be present in nature, even before humanity's emergence. Thus human beings must be preserved because they are the repository of a magnificent natural heritage which commits it to existence. Jonas thinks we must answer for mankind and the future world, in terms of a commitment to an infinite and universal plan of creation[127]. In short, ethics of responsibility requires that human beings respect a fundamental duty: to ensure the future of both nature and humanity under an obligation to the past that has originated both.

*Apel and Habermas*

The Karl-Otto Apel and Jürgen Habermas dialogical ethics emphasizes the co-responsibility concept as a starting point for the post metaphysical transformation of Kantian philosophy. This idea is the articulating core of the discourse ethics proposal. In the

---

[126] In this sense, it would not be foolish to ask whether the extra-human nature - enthralled by the technological apparatus - raises in itself a moral demand for tis own moral right.

[127] Jonas, Hans, *Das Prinzip Veranwortung: Versuchi einer Ethic für die Tecnologische Zivilisation*, Francfort am Main, Insel Verlag, 1988, p. 72.

*Critique of Pure Reason*, Kant asks what would be the conditions of possibility to a valid knowledge. To answer he introduces the separation between a noumenal world (the thing in itself) that is unknowable, and a phenomenal world that is presented to consciousness. Apel and Habermas do not need to draw on this distinction, because in their ethics, the starting point of reflection migrates from individual consciousness to language that can, in principle, be shared by all.

All those who are endowed with communicative competence, that is not only to understand, agree and interpret, are valid interlocutors. Therefore, the central question of dialogical ethics, unlike Kant, is: Are there conditions of possibility of intersubjective agreement about the truth and the meaning of statements? The answer is yes. However, all interlocutors will share the responsibility for their actions and their consequences in society. The mere use of language and the presence of conventional rules, show to the interlocutor its belonging (that it belongs) to a community. The "I think" of Kant refers to a philosophy of consciousness, based on the Cartesian *Cogito Ergo Sum*. Instead, in Apel and Habermas that *Cogito* becomes a "We argue".

Here arises the question about the relation between discourse ethics and the historical responsibility of ethics for its own application. In this regard, in "Über Moralität und Sittlichkeit" Habermas proposed the formulation of principle of universalization (U):

(U) A [moral norm] is valid just in case the foreseeable consequences and side-effects of its general observance for the interests and value-orientations of *each individual* could be *jointly* accepted by *all* concerned without coercion (i.e., in a sufficiently reasonable discourse).

This principle would replace Kant's categorical imperative, and would mean, only in a partial and fragmentary way, a discursive and post metaphysical transformation of Kant's philosophy. At first, (U) would be able to respond to the joint liability (Joint responsibility) demands and the global impact of the current collective activities, unlike the Kantian imperative that requires a kind of mental experiment, through which to discern what maxims are universalizable. In front of this requirement, discourse ethics orders speakers to participate in real discourses. Then, through those speeches the rules that will be valid for all who have participated on equal terms in its formulation, are defined by consensus.

However, it follows that (U) is not sufficient to ensure that consensus. According to Apel, this principle should and could be applied to the regulation of conflicts, which in practice is impossible without addressing necessary exceptions in its application. This philosopher proposes a principle of complementarily reciprocity (C), which commands collaboration for progressive installation of possibility conditions of (U). Therefore, (C), would be a formal principle (its delivery, not content) which would act as a regulative idea of a teleological action; namely, it would be putting into practice a kind of moral strategy, which from an accountability point of view, would protect the environment from risks involved in an unrestricted and arbitrary application of (U). Then, (C) would be a teleological principle that would reveal the true claim of universality of discourse ethics. If it is not recognized, we might assume that doctrines such as Human Rights could be applied only in the Western world (where there are conditions for its implementation). Therefore, the recognition of this principle implies an acceptance of a responsibility which requires speakers to assist in its implementation in speaking communities[128].

From the real community of communication survival, (C) represents a condition of possibility for ideal community emergence. This ethic of responsibility emphasizes the complementary nature of deontology and teleology. That is, it recognizes both as convergent, in the context of Western moral reasoning, the history of the late twentieth century. Therefore, the ethic of responsibility, both of Habermas and Apel, tends to break down the subject-object paradigm of modernity that leads to the division between people and world. This is proved under the close relationship between our destiny as social beings and the preservation of public space, understood as a place eminently argumentative. This idea not only represents a bioethics possibility condition but, above all, indicates the individual is a being-in-the-world, whose welfare is unthinkable if is not accompanied by the good in the world consideration.

*Engelhardt*

In an effort to elucidate the basic bioethical problems of pluralistic and secular societies, Engelhardt centers its efforts in identifying the basic principles that govern the possibility of communication and

[128]See, Apel, Karl-Otto, 1993.

collaboration between morally-strange secular communities, that is, communities with different moral viewpoints, values and principles. These problems have an immense importance since, according to Engelhardt, they are the conflict "at the roots of bioethics."[129]

He introduces the principles of permission and beneficence, which are at the base of all ethical relationships between morally strange communities, by introducing them presented as "the source, beginnings, commencements or origins of particular areas of the moral life."[130] Even though they are not "fundamental", at least they are useful in moral deliberation and the solution of ethical issues.Thereby, Engelhardt assumes *a priori* that human beings reject force as being a solution for ethical differences.

The principle of permission states the limits in the interaction between different morally strange individuals and communities. Only through authorization (willful agreement of parts involved) can one act involving others due to the impossibility of stating a binding rational universal morality in a secular society. [131] Since differences in values and viewpoints are inescapable, only through valid permit we can act affecting others, the moral strangers:

> The moral fabric sustaining the various forms of the moral life is then a general practice that is as unavoidable as is the interest in resolving moral disputes. In terms of that morality, mutual respect

---

[129] Engelhardt, JR. Tristam H., *The Foundations of Bioethics*. Second Edition, Oxford University Press, 1996, p. 103.

[130] Ibid., p.103.

[131] Ibid., p.124.

> becomes understood as using others only with their permission.[132]

This principle also states the authority to decide whether a particular moral action is good or bad. However, it neither entails a general binding understanding of morality nor intends to establish one. Since general agreements of what is right and wrong cannot be meeting, either "through rational arguments or common beliefs,"[133] the authority to decide and sanction what is wrong or right is left to what is agreed between parts in the particular case. Now, if actions are done against authorized acts, one *can* expect licit (but not mandatory) retaliation by force from the offended. These sanctions for immorality are justified because we commit to a "peaceable society" as soon as we start talking about moral communication across moral communities. Thus, violating the principle of permission justify "circumscription of the autonomy of the offender" as a punitive answer to his acts.[134] One should also expect the consequence of being set aside of that moral community due to that misbehavior. In general terms:

> The Principle of Permission is the necessary condition for the possibility of resolving moral disputes between moral strangers with moral authority and for sustaining

---

[132] Ibid., p.104.
[133] Ibid., p.123.
[134] Ibid., p.111.

> a minimum secular ethical language of praise and blame. It is in this sense, formal.[135]

On the other hand, the principle of beneficence is related to the goal of morality, namely, to *do* the good and *avoid* the bad. Humans, as social animals, always participate in communities with diverse moral contents and when doing so, if one desires to be morally right one must act in a beneficent way and "do to others their good."[136] Thus, this principle "reflects the circumstance that moral concerns encompass the pursuit of goods and the avoidance of harms."[137] Beneficence has an important role in unveiling a characteristic of human nature, as we tend to state our goals in social terms, involving others, and it is there that differences express. Beneficence is the bone and flesh of morality, "because without a commitment to beneficence the moral life has no content,"[138] and it "grounds what can be termed the morality of welfare and social sympathies."[139]

Sanctions for immoral actions at the level of the principle of beneficence can only be intellectual; if one has failed to act beneficently according to one moral community "one has at most cut oneself off from the beneficent community."[140]

Engelhadrt then forwards a question concerning malevolence, understood as an action against beneficence. What happens to those

[135] Ibid., p.109.
[136] Ibid., p.124.
[137] Ibid., p. 123.
[138] Ibid., p. 123.
[139] Ibid., p. 124.
[140] Ibid., p. 109.

that *act malevolently*? If such is the case, acting against the good of a community or individual, but with permission, should not be answered with force, since permission is the basis for secular morality. Now, if the case is that the action is done without permission and against the good of an individual or community, the offender must surely be answered with force since he/she is not legitimized to act in such way.

Due to the nature of these principles, Engelhardt states that permission is "conceptually prior to beneficence."[141] One can imagine a situation in which one would actually violate the principle of permission without even knowing what concept of beneficence is present in that particular community, "one can act in non-beneficient ways without being in conflict with the minimal notion of morality."[142]

Regarding to another principle of bioethics that has been put forward by authors such as Beauchamp and Childress,[143] called principle of justice, claims on it are also seen by Engelhardt as being "at root a concern with beneficence,"[144] since those judgments of justice presuppose a particular content-rich viewpoint. Bioethical matters such as health care resource allocation and physician-patient relationships are taken into consideration by this appeals to justice ("*what ought to be done*") and are part of the global moral issues.

---

[141] Ibid., p.124.
[142] Ibid., p.105.
[143] Beauchamp, T and Childress, J. *Principles of Biomedical Ethics*. Sixth Edition, Oxford University Press, New York, Oxford, 2009.
[144] Ibid., p. 121.

In relation to the socio-political implications of these principles, Engelhardt thinks that we need to secure basis for a neutral democracy that commits itself "to not being committed to a particular vision of the good."[145] Democracies should focus on allowing individuals and communities the fulfillment of personal values and ends, as long as these respect the minimum right of other individuals and communities of not being acted upon without authorization and allowing them too the pursuit of their own "good." Until now, the rules of traditional ethics have sought to regulate human relationships. It is now, however, that we should keep in mind the valuative, ideological, religious and philosophical discrepancies that can be seen in globalization. This axiological diversity involves generating procedures to ensure tolerance and respect for our differences, in addition to forming a basis for recognizing, on behalf of moral strangeness, a certain minimum of morality that would allow protecting the equality of human beings in the exercise of their rights and fulfillment of their duties. At this point, evidently bioethics has a relevant responsibility.

Contemporary societies are diverse and complex. These characteristics ought to be included in the current bioethical debate. Otherwise, it will not be possible to generate a theoretical platform that could allow for the procedurization and foundation of moral standards that would help overcome the valuative gap opened by the technological phenomenon and moral strangers.

---

[145] Ibid., p.120.

*Analitical Pluralism*

The democratic societies of the second half of the twentieth century have characterized themselves for having a critical attitude; namely the "axiological polytheism" which, as we recall, means that given the diversity of moral concepts, we must all have equal value. This denies the possibility of displaying and demonstrating the universal validity of some of them. The acceptance of one value or another would be conditioned exclusively by an emotional factor that is of a subjective and individual nature.[146]

Given the existing cultural diversity and different views of what is considered to be good in contemporary societies "moral strangers" have emerged. Thus, bioethics should focus its efforts on complementing two aspirations, which are apparently irreconcilable, but equally essential for creating decent and adequate conditions for social coexistence: to elucidate a basis for universally accepted standards, and to achieve the consolidation of respect for the different values, which are inherent in human nature.

Along with the meritorious and legitimate right of differences, every society needs to consolidate a common moral foundation which, in turn, justifies not only the right but also the duty to respect these differences. Moreover, one of the most interesting attempts to obtain a procedural key that would allow for the adequate coexistence of culturally diverse and morally distant individuals has been pluralism. While this ethic responds to different programmatic variants and currents, you may note that, in broad strokes, they agree on proposing, more or less, the following.

146 See: Weber, Max, *Le Savant et le Politique*, Paris, Éditions La Découverte, 2003.

Pluralism, typical of Western democratic societies, does not guarantee tolerance in an *a priori* way. According to Berlin, however, rejecting it implies an incentive to develop its natural opposite: intolerance. This, because if one denies the existence of a diversity of moral values and moral weighting, some irreconcilable with each other, promotes the possibility of imposing, on the rest of the individuals, a set of values that is considered correct.[147] In the reverse sense, subscribing to pluralism fosters respect and understanding of a legitimate diversity of values. However, this does not necessarily justify the respect for ideas, beliefs and different or contrary practices, and only in the last part of the twentieth century it has become sort of a requirement for the reflection of contemporary moral philosophy. In this context, autonomy, understood in the Kantian sense, has become a key concept for pluralism. Raz would observe that because of the wide range of values that hold a society together, pluralism seeks to determine those that should be guarded and promoted, and those that must, at all costs, be rejected.[148] I think this choice involves an inherent problem for pluralism: the competition between the different values that claim legitimacy.

How can this problem be tackled? Raz believes to have found the answer within the relationship that exists between tolerance and autonomy. Tolerance is necessary to society for two reasons: the diversity of individuals and their interest in exercising their autonomy. In my view, the danger here is that under such autonomy

147 See: Berlin Isaiah, *Four Essays on Liberty*, Oxford University Press, 1969.
148 Raz, Joseph, *The Morality of Freedom*, Oxford, Clarendon Press, 1986, pp. 67ff.

some might seek to impose their own values, only for considering them to be better or more correct than others.
In my opinion, pluralism is justified and, in turn, bases itself on dialectic: the *thesis* of the moral diversity which under the constitution of modern democratic societies requires the reconciliation of these differences, aims at a *synthesis* that integrates them with the *antithesis* which shows an ideal of life that is based on a single set of values. I see pluralism as an applied ethics, precisely because of its clear intention to not only justify, but to provide a methodology for human relationships as bioethics also pretends.

## II.3. Principles of Biomedical Ethics

Principles of biomedical ethics have changed since their first appearance in 1979. Beauchamp and Childress have expanded their content by reworking weak points and clarifying contradictory notions. I am specifically working with the sixth edition of their seminal book which also contains new elements. The authors have added an entirely new chapter on the Moral Status, extending the theory and fundamentals of common morality considering phenomena such as globalization for the analysis of the principle of justice and taking into account the recent theoretical debate whether or not to give greater depth and meaning to the nonmaleficence principle. However, as we shall see, the essential architecture of its postulates remains unaffected.

Beauchamp and Childress emphasize that moral conflicts of scientific and medical practice should be approached from two levels: the level of principles and the level of standard rules. Principles have a general, theoretical and abstract character. Rules have a particular, practical and concrete nature. Thus, the principles imply fundamentals, definitions and further, define the epistemological scope of deliberation. For its part, the rules represent the procedural level which must be applied to all moral reasoning.

However, going from the principles to the rules is very complicated. So far, the principles represent only deliberate references or, in other words, counsel to the consciousness and common sense of those involved. The rules, despite having a more limited and specific scope, do not have a binding value; that is, they do not force people beyond the realm of ethics. This complex dichotomy has led me to think about a possibility which exceeds the objectives of this essay. For this reason, I will not discuss it here but I will leave it raised: the eventual need for juridifying bioethics.

Beauchamp and Childress order their principles as follows: Respect for Autonomy, Nonmaleficence, Beneficence and Justice. I do not claim an exhaustive analysis of them, because I might enlarge much. My intention, in this occasion, is to reveal some theoretical problems of principlism, which in my opinion, require clarification or at least discussion in pursuit of expanding the understanding of bioethics. Furthermore, I intend to provide more and better elements for moral deliberation on complex issues that have arisen with the technological development and with the new paradigms of globalization.

*Respect for Autonomy*

(Originally *Autonomy*) Protects the every human being's right to act or allow acting on it, fully informed of potential risks, consequences and damage that such action might implicate. However, at the same time, autonomy states the obligation to respect that right, which because of the intrinsic definition of this principle will become a difficult problem for principlism.

Beauchamp and Childress say:

> Although we begin our discussion of principles of biomedical ethics with respect for autonomy, our order of presentation does not imply that this principle has moral priority over other principles. We do not hold, as some critics suggest, that the principle for respect for autonomy overrides all other moral considerations. Furthemore, we attempt to show that, in a properly structured theory, respect for autonomy is not excessively individualistic (thereby neglecting the social nature of individuals and the impact of individual choices and actions on others), not excessively focused on reason (thereby neglecting the emotions) and not unduly legalistic (thereby highlighting legal rights and downplaying social practices and responsabilities).[149]

[149] Beauchamp, T. and Childress, J., *Principles of Biomedical Ethics,* Sixth Edition, New York-Oxford, Oxford University Press, 2009, p. 99.

Thus, we can see in this principle two basic requirements of freedom which are shared by several doctrinal currents: individual autonomy and intentionality. Autonomy implies a power and an appetite; namely, the ability to make decisions and the will to do it. This means that autonomy require a certain understanding on the value of choice. On the other hand, intentionality involves a deliberative consciousness and the capacity for self-determination.
Now, the renaming of this principle deserves some consideration. Beauchamp and Childress realized that the original principle of autonomy led to many controversies, mainly since it could be understood as the absolute freedom of the patient to decide and impose his decision. However, that does not happen in practice because of the paternalistic culture of science and medicine. Many times the decisions of patients, when they were inconsistent with the decisions of scientists and doctors, are not taken into account. Thus, to establish a greater consistency between theory and the actual practice of the principle, Beauchamp and Childress narrowed the epistemological and procedural scope of principle by renaming it "Respect for Autonomy."
Therefore, the authors argue that we should not understand individual autonomy as an absolute and unilateral power, but as a capability or competence characterized by detailed information, understanding of the essential things and absence of coercion[150]. However, the absence of coercion is just a procedural feature of the

[150] For the concept of competence, see Beauchamp, T. and Childress, J., *Principles of Biomedical Ethics*, Sixth Edition, New York-Oxford, Oxford University Press, 2009, p. 112-117.

principle because on a practical level, a decision made in an informed, comprehensive and free way might be contradicted by another agent, since that decision might violate other principles which, in a given case, might have more value than individual autonomy.

Thereby, respect for autonomy not only establishes a binding obligation (which the authors call a positive obligation) but also the individual right of the patient to be independent in his decisions, implicit in what Beauchamp and Childress call negative obligation.[151]

> The fundamental requirement is to respect a particular person's autonomous choices, whatever they may be. Respect for autonomy is not a mere *ideal* in health care; it is a professional *obligation*. Autonomous choice is a *right* – not a *duty* – of patients.[152]

This allows for the individual right, under certain conditions, to be contradicted.

*Nonmaleficence*

This principle superimposes the moral obligation of not doing evil over doing good. Moreover, it shows that duty is to never hurt,

---

[151] For *negative* obligation and *positive* obligation, see Beauchamp, T. and Childress, J., *Principles of Biomedical Ethics,* Sixth Edition, New York-Oxford, Oxford University Press, 2009, p. 104-105.

[152] Beauchamp, T. and Childress, J., *Principles of Biomedical Ethics,* Sixth Edition, New York-Oxford, Oxford University Press, 2009, p. 107.

either physically or morally, human beings, and to avoid, at all costs, actions that may involve some damage to them.

The first point is very important, and Beauchamp and Childress stress it:

> Obligations not to harm others are sometimes more stringent than obligations to help them, but the reverse is also true. If in a particular case a health care provider inflicts a very minor injury (swelling from a needlestick, say), then we consider the obligation of beneficence to take priority over the obligation of nonmaleficence. The point is that causing some risks of surgical harm, introducing social costs to protect the public health, and placing burdens on some research subjects can all be justified by the benefits of the actions.[153]

Based on the thesis of Frankena, Beauchamp and Childress make a distinction between Nonmaleficence and Beneficence, because they think the two principles can not be understood as one. Frankena divides the principle of beneficence into four general obligations (which in some cases may be ranked depending of the specific situation):

1. One ought not to inflict evil or harm (what is bad).
2. One ought to prevent evil or harm.
3. One ought to remove evil.

[153] Ibid., p. 150.

4. One ought to do or promote good.[154]

Beauchamp and Childress agreed with the enunciation of these obligations, but they do not beleive that all of them mean beneficence. Their main reason is that they do not understand the obligation of doing good as morally equivalent with the obligation of not doing harm. In this sense, the first obligation would be more binding than the other three, because it implies the duty of never inflicting harm or hurting someone; namely, to respect the maxim *primum non nocere*.[155] Therefore, they rearranged the obligations as follows:

Nonmaleficence

1. One ought not to inflict evil or harm.

Beneficence

2. One ought to prevent evil or harm.
3. One ought to remove evil or harm.
4. One ought to do or promote good.[156]

The obligation of not doing harm implies a moral correctness criterion which is higher than the obligation of simply doing good. However, the intention of Beauchamp and Childress is not to support a superiority of the principle of nonmaleficence over

---

[154] Frankena, William, *Ethics*, Second Edition, New Jersey, Prentice Hall, 1973, p. 47.
[155] Beauchamp, T. and Childress, J., *Principles of Biomedical Ethics*, Sixth Edition, New York-Oxford, Oxford University Press, 2009, p. 149.
[156] Ibid., p. 151.

beneficence but to explain that the obligation of doing good is epistemologically and procedurally related to the obligation of not doing evil. In my view, this creates a complex problem and a clear contradiction. Let's see.

Sometimes, the obligation of doing good may be tragically contradicted with the obligation of not doing evil since both involve principles that are *prima facie*. Therefore, we lack, at least in theory, some plausible criterion to rank them. While there is a tendency to consider more binding the principle of nonmaleficence, it is also true that in many cases is more reasonable to first apply the principle of beneficence: Can we force the patient to bear the heavy burden of treatment (nonmaleficence) to preserve his life (beneficence), at the cost of an acute and constant suffering and relentless deterioration? Is there a contradiction between the right to dignity (dignified life) and the duty to protect, preserve and promote life? Should physicians continue that kind of treatment, at any cost, regardless of the will of the patient? Is a disproportionate medical treatment that only prolongs the agony of terminally ill patients legitimate? If the therapeutical means are useless or ineffective and their application causes the patient acute suffering, must we continue with them until the end? Is death always harmful? If we respond to these questions affirmatively, we would have to accept that nonmaleficence is, *a priori* and by definition, superior to beneficence since the obligation of not harming would imply a greater moral objectivity than doing good, because it would protect higher values like life. However, in some circumstances, these values could be transformed into abstract concepts whose dogmatic and intolerant defense could cause great suffering to a person. In other words, the principle of nonmaleficence may end up denying itself, namely infringing in practice what in theory it protects.

Therefore, nonmaleficence and beneficence could only be justified as separate principles if we understand the first one as a duty, and the second one as an individual right. Thus, the collision between them could be resolved by imposing nonmaleficence over beneficence, because the former implies binding obligations which are grounded in the protection and promotion of universally accepted values, eg, life. Therefore, under certain circumstances, an individual could be required to waive his right to beneficence because his particular understanding about what good is can not prevail over what has been socially agreed as such. Otherwise, if we consider both nonmaleficence and beneficence as duties, it will be very difficult to find plausible criteria to rank them when they come into conflict.

*Beneficence*

Beneficence implies that every person is ensured to receive appropriate care. For Beauchamp and Childress the essence of morality is contained in this principle: doing good. This duty is not only a conventional obligation but part of human nature and an esential tendency of human beings. However, beneficence, besides being a personal option, is also an obligation. In this sense, these authors attempt to separate the concept of beneficence from benevolence, understanding the former not merely as an act of charity or an ideal of virtue, but as the positive duty to:

1. Protect and defend the rights of others.
2. Prevent harm from occurring to others.
3. Remove conditions that will cause harm to others.
4. Help persons with disabilities.
5. Rescue persons in danger.[157]

Nevertheless, these obligations are not absolute, because each individual could only partially fulfill them; that is, no one is capable of doing all the good that is possible to do. Beauchamp and Childress emphasize this ambiguous character of Beneficence and recognize that "the line between an obligation and moral ideal is often unclear".[158] The case of rule number (1) is eloquent. To protect and defend the rights of others means to defend their autonomy and will. This implies defending their individual and inalienable right of following a particular life project based on what each person understands by good. However, in the case of principlism we have to understand individual rights as a heteronomous concept; that is, as a prerogative that people cannot perform nor choose by themselves because beneficence is a right that is determined by other criteria which do not necessarily match with the involved person. This situation is justified by the paternalism doctrine since, in certain cases, when a patient is in an evident risk of suffering harm, it could be warranted to restrict his autonomy and to contradict his personal understanding of beneficence in order to protect him and to respect

[157] Ibid., p. 199.
[158] Ibid., p. 199.

the duty of always doing good for the patient.[159] In this sense, the principle of Beneficence stresses its status of duty over its category of right.[160]

Beauchamp and Childress also distinguish between *Positive beneficence* and utility. *Positive beneficence* requires that the action produces benefits and the presence of an agent who benefits others. *Utility beneficence* requires a reasonable balance between risks and benefits involved. However, this distinction shows us that Beauchamp and Childress consider two principles of beneficence where the agent is more important than the patient:

> *Positive beneficence* requires agents to provide benefits to others. *Utility beneficence* requires that agents balance benefits, risks, and costs to produce the best overall results.[161]

Therefore, we find here a very transcendental problem to bioethical deliberation which can be posed as a question: Who decides what the good is, the patient or the agent? Is Paternalism acceptable in all

---

[159] For paternalism and hard paternalism, see: Beauchamp, T. and Childress, J., *Principles of Biomedical Ethics,* Sixth Edition, New York-Oxford, Oxford University Press, 2009, p. 213-216.

[160] An example of this is the Chilean case of a patient who suffering of a terminal cancer, refused to continue with chemotherapy, fully informed, aware of his decision and its consequences. He made that decision by considering as a benefit to finish with the suffering associated with chemotherapy; also, the treatment was useless. However, doctors considered beneficial - and a duty – to continue the treatment and prolong the life of the patient as much as possible (regardless of his will and suffering). For this reason, they presented a protective action in the Chilean courts to force him to continue the "treatment"; that legal action was accepted with the judges.

[161] Beauchamp, T. and Childress, J., *Principles of Biomedical Ethics,* Sixth Edition, New York-Oxford, Oxford University Press, 2009, p. 197.

cases? Does every human being have the right to freely consider what is good for him, and believe, practice and hold a truth from his cultural and religious identity?

In my view, the obligation to do good must be linked to the obligation to protect and promote the legitimate interests of the affected person. It is clear that we cannot force an alive and healthy person to donate his heart to another individual to save that other individual's life. Nor is it plausible to force someone to give all their property to help many more people who live in poverty. In the same way, it should be clear that in certain circumstances, we should not force individuals to go beyond what they consider good for themselves. That would imply the imposition of supererogatory obligations which are not always legitimate. Thereby, there are circumstances in which it is much more reasonable to respect what each person considers to be good and not to objectify in a paternalistic way the principle of beneficence. Otherwise, the intrinsic definition of the principle of beneficence would reveal a kind of sophism, or at least, a paraconsistent argumentation.

Beneficence implies an altruistic act; namely, thinking about the other, and thus means to do the good for the patient where the good is sometimes what the patient thinks is good for himself. Therefore, the simple fact of accepting beneficence as a kind of altruism can show us the ambiguity of this principle. Sometimes, paternalism is justified. Sometimes, it is not.

*Justice*

This principle emphasizes the duty to protect a human being from any kind of discrimination that violates his identity, dignity and status as an end in himself, and thus always treats him as an equal. The main orientation of this principle must be to recognize the equality among human beings. However, it is necessary to clarify the requirements of this equality, recognizing, at least, three basic rights that involve the duty to respect them: 1. The right to a physically and psychologically healthy life, 2. The right of access to a proper, adequate and timely medical attention, and 3. The right to have equal opportunities to access the healthcare system.

Nevertheless, and due to the absence of a social consensus about diverse theories of justice, the analysis becomes very complicated. The authors recognize, at least, six kinds of distributive justice, adding the sixth one with respect to the Belmont Report:

1. To each person an equal share.
2. To each person according to need.
3. To each person according to effort.
4. To each person according to contribution.
5. To each person according to merit.
6. To each person according to free-market exchanges.[162]

Many theories accept these six principles as valid. Beauchamp and Childress also do so, noting that each of them represents a *prima facie* obligation that is not hierarchical with respect to the others.

[162] Ibid., p. 243.

But as this scheme is a theoretical framework for understanding the principle of justice, is a reference of a general character which is inexorably going to find serious problems in its application to moral problems which are always of a particular nature. The problem then is to determine which one has more value over another in certain circumstances. Beauchamp and Childreess do not consider it possible to accomplish this task without reviewing some classical theories in order to specify and balance these obligations. Thus, they complete a cursory analysis of Utilitarian, Libertarian, Communitarian and Egalitarian theories.[163] While they clarify that they are using these theories as a methodological resource and claim to seek a complementation between these theoretical approaches, they probably have a predilection for Rawl's theory of justice, which implies, according the authors, two main principles: 1. Each individual's liberty must be compatible, in a similar measure, with the liberty of others, and 2. The fair equality of opportunity must be assured to can accept inequalities in social primary goods.[164] However, Rawls's conception, whatever is its theoretical value, does not resolve the practical problem of balancing the different principles of distributive justice. In this way, the criterion to rank those diverse obligations and rights keep its relative character. Therefore, this understanding of the principle of justice implies a risk that apparently the authors have not considered: the danger of turning principlism into a casuistry theory in which "the case by

[163] Ibid., p. 244-248.
[164] Ibid., 2009, p. 247.

case" would determine which obligations and rights have precedence over others.

I think that the model chosen by Beauchamp and Childress to support the principle of justice is unable to provide a ranking of the topics that comes into play to resolve a conflict. This model allows us to establish only provisional conclusions regarding rights and depending on each particular case; namely, it leads us to what I call an extreme casuistry.

Therefore, if the principle of justice would be based on casuistic determinations it would no longer properly be a principle because it would have lost its status of theoretical framework, argumentative approach and deliberative structure. Justice would be a criterion based on an excessive confidence in common sense, and would represent an inductive model that went from the particular (the specific case) to the general (the principle), and would not give us certainty about the reasonable application of deliberative criteria. It would be a consequentialist and empiricist model rather than a rationalist structure.

Thereby, the authors understand the principle of justice as a deontological principle which implies an inalienable obligation of treating all individuals equally, beyond their particular condition. In my understanding, this means that we should accept that the principle of justice is superior to the other three, since this principle would not tolerate internal contradiction. If we do not understand it in this way, the principle becomes a relativized criterion and loses the unity of its content depending of the whims of each circumstance. Obviously this impasse needs to be thought out more carefully. However, the problem does not end here. The only way to ground a deontological principle of justice is by appealing to an ontological argument; that is, recognizing an inherent equality between all human beings regardless of their merit, need or contribution to society.

# III. PROBLEMS

## III.1. Critiques of Principlism

Several critiques have emerged against principlism. These critiques abound, but not all of them are relevant. On this occasion and before offering my own proposal, I would like to stress four of them: Jonsen and Toulmin's casuistic criticism, Daniel Callahan's, Danner Clouser and Bernard Gert's, and European Biolaw doctrine's represented by Jacob Dahl Rendtorff and Peter Kemp which offer four different principles. I will also give some arguments to refuse some of those critiques.

Principles and rules enjoy a privileged theoretical status in ethics. They are widely regarded as being "exhaustive of ethics, that is, as though all that moral understanding requires is a commitment to some code of rules, which can be accepted as authoritative."[165] In this sense, ethical problems faced daily are solved by adhering to a determined set of rules or values and adjusting our actions to it. According to Jonsen and Toulmin, such approach to moral

[165] Jonsen, Albert and Toulmin, Stephen, *The Abuse of Casuistry,* University of California Press, 1988, p. 5.

deliberation is incomplete. Principles and rules are not to be understood as the beginning and end of moral decision makings, instead, they urge us to think the possibility of facing moral quandaries with a different approach in mind – the "casuistic approach –," so that we may be set free of the "tyranny of principles."[166]

To completely grasp the idea of "casuistry vs. principles" the authors present an excellent example.[167] A young woman, who was struggling with her rent and food in order to help herself reach the end of the month afloat, started working in a telephone answering service. This job got her the money she needed to pay for her expenses. There was only one problem: she was also receiving social security payments (which were insufficient to cover all her needs, hence she started the phone service). Once the Social Security Office found out of this activity, which she did not inform to the Office, they ceased all payment for concepts of social security and made her even repay money for she was classified as a case of "welfare fraud." A male news reporter who was covering her story said about this case "There should be a *rule* to prevent this kind of thing from happening."[168] Jonsen and Toulmin stressed that he did not say there should be more "discretion", more "equity" or more "flexibility" in the application of rules he outright said there should be *a rule* for covering such a case. This kind of thinking implies that "Justice [...] is ensured only by establishing an adequate system of

[166] Ibid., pp.5-6.
[167] Ibid., p. 8.
[168] Ibid., p.9.

rules, so as to prevent such inequities from happening again in the future."[169] Actually, the authors note, principles can only do so much for moral deliberation, as seen in this example, where it is clear that what was needed was more wisdom rather than more rules. All decision making moral cases are in need of "perceptiveness" and "discernment," "and the more problematic the situations become, the greater is the need for such discernment."[170] Thereby, principles by themselves cannot suffice in moral practical decision-making for rules cover only unique situations contemplated expressly in them. Therefore, when cases depart from the paradigmatic case contained in the rule or law, the rule or law proves unhelpful since it does not contain a solution for a case that it does not contemplate.

As an answer to this central problem in ethics, Jonsen and Toulmin try to revitalize an old tradition, that is, the tradition of "casuistry," which has been in disrepute for hundreds of years, especially since the attacks Pascal fired unto Casuists in the mid-seventeenth century. "Casuistry" is described succinctly by the authors as "a reasonable and effective set of practical procedures for resolving the moral problems that arise in particular real-life situations."[171]

But what happened to this centuries-old tradition? Why did casuistry suddenly fall into oblivion? Why does it suffer such a bad reputation among contemporary intellectuals? Jonsen and Toulmin set forward to answer these questions, and subsequently, clean the name of "case ethics" or "casuistics." As an interesting fact, these authors note that

[169] Ibid., p. 9.
[170] Ibid., p. 9.
[171] Ibid., p. 10.

the Oxford English Dictionary has an accurate definition of casuistry but, it does also comment that the word's use was "apparently at first contemptuous" and it cites as relevant quotations three sources which question its value.[172]

As said, it was Blaise Pascal that delivered the finishing blow of casuistry with his *Provincial Letters.* Being the influential intellectual he was at his time, his pen would prove the end of casuistry as his influence on readers was all it took to disrepute casuistry completely. On the *Letters*, Pascal directly addressed the problems of the abuse of casuistry, since, at that time, he argued, casuistry was used by the French Jesuits for justifying unduly and partial treatment to those of their penitents that were wealthy or highborn. Interestingly enough, the authors hold, Pascal is obscure in this point, for it is not quite clear if he intended to attack "bad" casuistry only (the abuse of casuistry for the benefit of some privileged group or individual) or to attack the casuistic system as a whole.[173]

Another important historical blow to casuistry was delivered by philosopher Henry Sidgwick in his book *The Methods of Ethics* in 1874. Herein Sigwick proposed the departure from case analysis in ethics to a more general and theoretical approach to ethical and "meta-ethical" theory.

However it may be particular case-analysis keeps intact today in daily life decision makings. Jonsen and Toulmin maintain that although in highly-intellectual circles casuistry has been almost

[172] Ibid., p. 11.
[173] Ibid., p.15.

completely disdained – except for some two noteworthy examples, Sissela Bok's book *Lying* and Michael Walzers's book *Just and Unjust wars*[174] -, we have not forgotten its use in our regular lives. Therefore, casuistry is not dead, it is only sleeping.

Daniel Callahan has profusely criticized principlism giving interesting arguments in different parts of his work. However, one of his papers published in 2003 in *Perspectives in Biology and Medicine* has especially called my attention. In that paper, Callahan provides, in a few lines, a central argument summarizing his position about principlism.[175]

Following Aristotle and Hume, Callahan emphasizes the fact that human beings are social animals and, therefore, share the same nature that makes us seek and prefer social cohesion before solipsism and individualism. In this sense, Beauchamp and Childress' principlism has ignored the communitarian doctrine as a valid alternative for deliberation on biomedical problems which often involve not only the affected persons but the entire social group. According Callahan, bioethical issues cannot and should not be reduced neither to a matter of individual autonomy nor a circumstantial and casuistic decision-making. In this sense, bioethical principlism has forgotten public interest and has systematically delayed true moral good; namely, common good, the only one that can be justified in terms of our nature beyond to understand our life as a mere atomic co-existence of social particles.

---

[174] Ibid., p. 13.

[175] Callahan, Daniel, "Individual Good and Common Good. A Communitarian Approach to Bioethics", in *Perspectives in Biology and Medicine*, 46, 4, Washington, DC, The John Hopkins University Press, 2003, p. 496-507.

Callahan thinks that principlism "is an expression of liberal individualism."[176] This means that Beauchamp and Childress' interpretation of *The Principles of Biomedical Ethics* is "classically liberal":

> Autonomy as interpreted by principlism enshrines the right to make one's own decisions, but assiduously avoids specifying a means of evaluating the ethical content of those decisions; nonmaleficence, aiming to protect patients from harm, is a variant of the autonomy principle, emphasizing negative liberty, the right of bodily noninterference; the point of justice as a principle is to ensure a sufficiently fair share of social and medical resources, such that individuals are free to make efficacious autonomous judgments in living their lives, unhampered by social inequities; and beneficence comes down to assisting people to be treated fairly and empowered to live their autonomous lives.[177]

According to Callahan, every principle admits a communitarian translation where common good is the main criterion of moral rightness and the basic guideline to make decisions. I agree. However, the problem of Callahan's argumentation is not his critique, which is very plausible, but the diagnosis that he makes and how implements his proposal. We will now see that this procedure is not logically consistent with his criticism. Callahan's critique is a

---

[176] Ibid., p.505.
[177] Ibid.

paraconsistent critique since he offers as a first premise the fact that bioethical principlism is an ideologized methodology, marked by liberal individualism which enshrines individual autonomy as the core of moral deliberation. All other principles would be subject to autonomy at the expense of what Hume called "social virtues" which give greater importance to common good and public interest.[178] However, when Callahan explicitly characterizes principlism as a liberal ideology, is tacitly assuming the presence of the most fundamental feature of modern liberalism in principlism: paternalism, in which individual autonomy is often constrained by social environment and external agents under precisely what has been called "common good." In this sense, Callahan recognizes that of the four principles, beneficence (defined as individual beneficence) has been the most neglected.[179] This obviously is nothing new and is possible to see it clearly in the writings of Hume and Mill, where individual autonomy must be sacrificed for the benefit of the most of people, under a liberal principle of pure utilitarianism which is quite paternalistic.

In terms of content, Callahan's solution; that is, his conclusion is correct but, in formal terms, is contradictory and, therefore, inconsistent. He criticizes the ideology of principlism, which is related to liberal individualism, offering the contrary ideology; namely, communitarianism. Callahan says that "liberal

---

[178] See, Hume, David, *An Enquiry Concerning the Principles of Morals*, USA, Wilder Publications, 2008.

[179] Callahan, Daniel, "Individual Good and Common Good. A Communitarian Approach to Bioethics", in *Perspectives in Biology and Medicine*, 46, 4, Washington, DC, The John Hopkins University Press, 2003, p. 505.

individualism works overtime to avoid substantive analysis and judgment. Communitarian goes in just the opposite direction, embracing the hardest and deepest questions about the right uses of medical knowledge and technology."[180] This means that Callahan cannot refute the ideological feature of principlism but only replaces one doctrine for another. Thereby, after Callahan's critique, principlism remains as ideological as before.[181]

Finally and although Callahan recognizes the authoritarian trait of liberal individualism, I think that is not enough to say that autonomy is the guiding principle of principlism. [182] By contrast, the eventual dictatorial profile of principlism is reflected in its paternalistic trait and it is this feature which, precisely, makes the procedure sometimes becomes logically inconsistent.

On their hand, Clouser and Gert affirm that principlism is mistaken about the nature of morality and misleading as to the foundations of ethics.[183] This means that principlism, as a practice of using principles instead of moral theory or particular moral rules, does not work as its defenders think. According Clouser and Gert, principlism is only a set of very general and vague names related to ethical considerations and moral problems but is not a practical guideline to action. *The Principles of Biomedical Ethics* are always in contradiction to each other and therefore do not have any

[180] Ibid., p. 506.
[181] Ibid.
[182] Ibid.
[183] Clouser, Danner and Gert, Bernard, "A Critique of Principlism", in *The Journal of Medicine and Philosophy*, Volume 15, Oxford University Press, 1990, p. 220.

systematic relationship between them because of their eclectic use of moral theory.[184]

Therefore, for Clouser and Gert, principlism neither is a consistent ethical theory nor an effective deliberative process. *The Principles of Biomedical Ethics* are just a list of facts and considerations on various moral issues. Thus, they neither provide a plausible guide to action nor contain analogically consistent basis that comes from a clearly defined moral theory.

Under these arguments, Clouser and Gert seek to eliminate principlism, discrediting it not only as a method of bioethics but also as a general deliberative procedure, indicating that the most effective way to deliberate about moral problems is from a unified moral theory.[185]

I think Clouser and Gert's critique is too abstract and, therefore, is out of context with regard to the nature of bioethics. I will give three arguments to support my position. 1. If the path of principlism is to reason out about moral dilemmas, to deliberate on possible solutions for those problems, and finally to make decisions from a unified moral theory, this procedure is ignoring the eminently particular character of moral problems. Principlism was precisely conceived as a response to traditional moral theories, full of foundations but with a very limited scope and effectiveness in practice; that is, lacking of a procedural feature which is so necessary especially in the field of applied ethics. 2. Bioethics is eminently a trans-discipline; namely, many diverse but complementary disciplines converge in it. Thus,

[184] Ibid., p. 221.
[185] Ibid., p. 236.

bioethics is absolutely necessary to relate not only those different spheres of knowledge with each other but also different theoretical currents that provide foundations which, though come from different traditions, are very plausible. It is an empirically verifiable fact that current trend of ethics is to look for similarities between teleological and deontological elements of moral reasoning, considering them not as a weakness of the discipline but as its fortress. A general moral theory implies the risk to encapsulate human beings in a single mode of thought and to face them with the tragic dichotomy of choosing by ends or by duties as moral decision criteria, neglecting that, finally, ends and duties represent complementary theoretical approaches that strengthen rational deliberation and dialogue, and provide objectivity and impartiality to moral reasoning. The world-famous works of Hans Jonas, Karl-Otto Apel and Jurgen Habermas, among others, demonstrate the tendency which I am speaking about.[186] 3. Despite obstacles that bioethical principles have for their implementation, I think that it is unwise to ignore principlism. This deliberative procedure is not a matter related to good or bad philosophical taste. Nor it is a capricious and arbitrary methodology. In the complex field of moral reasoning,

---

[186] See: Jonas, Hans, *Das Prinzip Veranwortung: Versuchi einer Ethic für die Tecnologische Zivilisation*, Francfort am Main, Insel Verlag, 1988 (Jonas, Hans, *The imperative of responsibility. In Search of an Ethics for the Technological Age*, The University of Chicago Press, 1985). Apel, Karl-Otto, "Diskursethik als Ethik Mitveranwortung für kollektive Aktivitäten", en Hans-Joachim Waschkies, *Rehabilitierung des Subjektiven*. Festschrift für Hermann Schmitz, Bonn, Bouvier Verlag, 1993. Apel, Karl-Otto, "Fallibilismus.Konsenstheorie der Wahrheit und Letzbegründung", in *Philosophie und Begründung*, Frankfurt am Main, Suhrkamp, 1993. Habermas, Jürgen, *Technology and Science as Ideology, Toward a Rational Society*, Beacon Press, Boston, 1970. Habermas, Jürgen, "Wahrheitstheorien, en H. Fahrenbach (comp.), *Wirklichkeit und Reflexion*, Pfullingen, Neske, 1973.

principles represent a deliberative structure inherent in human reason, which is always in constant tension. Conflictivity is co-substantial to morality, and this conflictivity has been greatly enhanced and augmented due to the new moral problems, which has arisen as a result of globalization and biotechnology development. Principles not only represent possible answers to address those new dilemmas but also imply a reference to question eventual decisions which may be wrong since complexity that those problems involve.

Finally, it is wrong to think that only systematic approaches to moral problems bring good results. If so, philosophy and all kinds of reasoning about ethical and ontological dilemmas of humanity would have been expired with Hegel's tenets. In important moments of Western thought's history, conflicts and contradictions have been the best starting point for reflection. For proving this it is enough to remember the concept of *aporia* in Plato's *Sophist*, and the ontological category of *paradox* in the Kierkegaard's *Philosophical Fragments*. Principlism is not always a systematic and univocal procedure. However, we cannot conclude from that premise that it is inapplicable as deliberative methodology. *The Principles of Biomedical Ethics* are in constant tension and, usually, come into contradiction. This, principally, means two things: 1. Principlism requires dialogue, pacific argumentation and consensus between those involved; namely, is a pluralistic procedure, and 2. It represents an accurate reading of our nature.

On other hand, Rendtorff and Kemp recognize the roots of biolaw in bioethics but, at the same time, reject *The Principles of Biomedical Ethics* since those authors consider the concept of autonomy is not properly related to other principles of equal or greater importance, such as dignity, integrity and vulnerability. Rendtorff and Kemp think this situation debilítate Beauchamp and Childress' principlism.[187]

The doctrine of Biolaw has its starting point in these relationships and could not be justified without understand dignity, vulnerability and integrity as complementary principles of autonomy. However, that reasoning has a paraconsistent argument that biolaw must resolve and clarify as soon as possible. Understand autonomy as a capacity is not consistent with cenceive dignity as an intrinsic condition of human being. It is true that it is necessary to have certain skills and abilities to exercise autonomy, but autonomy neither is born nor justifies only with its exercise. The possibility to represent a person in his decisions and choices loses substrate and basis if autonomy ends when inability begins, even if this inability is circumstantial. Autonomy and dignity will have logical consistency only if both concepts are understood as inherent to human nature, that is, as inalienable rights that come with the same notion (or idea in the Platonic sense) of humanity, not with the ability to be autonomous or be worthy. Be free and be recognized in our dignity represent an ontological *a priori* and not an epistemological capacity because being an autonomous and dignified person does not depend on our merit, our social condition, our contribution to society or how much money we have. The issue here is whether we understand

---

[187] Rendtorff, Jacob Dahl and Kemp, Peter, *Basic Ethical Principles in European Bioethics and Biolaw*, Vol. I, Report to the European Commission of the BIOMED-II Project, Guissona (Catalunya), Spain, Centre for Ethics and Law (Copenhagen) and Institut Borrja de Bioetica (Barcelona), 2000, p. 19.

autonomy and dignity as inherent attributes of our humanity that make equal all human individuals regardless of their circumstances, or if we are going to understand that in the world there are human beings who are more free and more valuable than others.

Biolaw stresses that we should understand autonomy as the mixture between free choices and external influences which is in contradiction with the fact of thinking about autonomy as a capacity.[188] Moreover, if autonomy involves the ability of self-determination, the ability of self-legislation, of having privacy, of making rational decisions, the ability of participating politically in the public space, we must understand, then, that the prisoners have lost their abilities and not their rights. In this sense, I think the definition of autonomy requires a distinction between essential rights (those that make us equal as individuals) and legal rights (those that we can obtain and losses based on merit and conventions). It is also necessary to deepen the concept of legal equality and intrinsic equality. The prisoner has lost his legal rights and therefore is not legally like the rest of the individuals. He has not lost the ability to self-determination. He has lost the right to self-determination. He has not lost the ability to participate in politics. He has no longer the right to do it. At least, in theory, the prisoner remains intrinsically equal as other individuals. However, under these conventions that we call laws the prisoner has lost most of his rights but retaining his abilities. The prisoner has not lost the ability

[188] Ibid., p. 25.

to be free. He has lost the right to be free, the most important of human rights.

Finally, the principles of biolaw are tautological in respect of *The Principles of Biomedical Ethics*. The former do not extend the epistemological scope of the second. Dignity, vulnerability and integrity can be seen as implicitly contained in the principles of Beauchamp and Childress, especially in the principles of beneficence and nonmaleficence. In this sense, the critique of Rendtorff and Kemp does not overcome, either epistemologically or methodologically, the problem of principlism.

## III.2. The Problem of Principlism

I will give five general criticisms of Beauchamp and Childress principlism, with their corresponding arguments, in order to sustain and complete my previous statements.

1. *Absence of an objective criterion for ranking principles.* Principles are contradicted in practice and ranking them is not possible without recourse to consequentialist criteria. This diminishes deontological foundations of deliberation because those bases do not offer plausible elements to regulate, in certain specific cases, the general application of principles which may be harmful. The ethical principles structure does not admit exceptions in its application, creating a kind of "deaf dialogue" between groups that discuss sensitive issues such as the banning of religious displays in public space, free distribution of contraception pills, euthanasia, abortion or

the ontological status of the embryo, accusing each other of being "backward" or "murderers," as appropriate.

2. *Theoretical and practical divergence among the principles.* We cannot clearly know what criterion guides the application of principles. On formal terms, the deontological criterion does. But in practical terms, it is only what finally gives the content to bioethics; a utilitarian criterion guides it. Therefore, overcoming the divergence between teleology and deontology is not observable in principlism because consequentialist and hypothetical elements take precedence over the deontological and categorical principles. This suggests the need to find a criterion for prioritization of the principles. This criterion does not imply subordination, neither casuistic nor dogmatic of one principle to another, but complementariness each other.[189]
3. *Apparent neutrality of principles.* Beauchamp and Childress' principlism does not overcome the theoretical divergence between teleology and deontology; namely, the antinomy that makes us to think that we can only act or be moved by ends and consequences or by intentions and obligations. From a moral point of view, principlism was defined as a neutral procedure. However, that is not right. In theory, principlism has higher compatibility with the deontological branch of ethics, and stresses the superiority of universal and binding values over particular conceptions and

---

[189] Robert Veatch has examined how different ethical theories attempt to resolve conflicts among ethical principles. See: *The Basics of Bioethics*, Second Edition, New Jersey, Prentice Hall, 2003, p. 167 and following. For casuistic subordination, see: Jonsen, A. and Toulmin, S., *The Abuse of Casuistry. A History of Moral Reasoning*, University of California Press, 1989. Especially Parts IV, V and VI.

inclinations. On other hand, principlism follows a utilitarian reasoning in the concrete resolution of different moral conflicts. Therefore, its neutrality is only apparent.

4. *The principlism's procedure depends on contradicition.* Beauchamp and Childress' principlism is relativistic and it has a significant dependence of contradiction. Principlism gives general guidelines (the principles) which seek universality but, at the same time, it seems to accept exceptions in its application. Moreover, as the principles are theoretically equivalent, the criteria for ranking them are relativistic. The value of principles has a parasitical nature because that value depends on the absence of contradiction. If such contradiction is insurmountable, principles lose their objective value; that is, they lose their meaning and their significance since they are not already effective to resolve any moral problem; namely, they are no longer applicable and it is necessary to appeal to casuistry. The applicability of a principle is not due to its inherent ability to act as a deliberative criterion but represents a kind of accident (in the Aristotelian sense) of itself: namely, a temporary feature, which is subject to fact whether or not there is internal conflict between principles.[190]
5. *Principles have maintained their same definition along the time.* The definition and meaning of principles have remained the same despite the techno-scientific advances and the great changes of

[190] When I say "accident" I mean an attribute which can or cannot belong to a subject. In other words, a feature that is not essential or substantial in the entity. For the Aristotelian concept of accident, see: Aristotle, *Metaphysics*, New York, The Modern Library, 2001. Especially, V, 7-10, VI, 2 and XI, 8. Also, see: Aristotle, *Organon*, New York, The Modern Library, 2001. Especially, *Topica* I, 5.

globalization. Beuchamp and Childress have made an attempt to adjust their proposal to new conditions arising in the last twenty years. However, their theory and their procedure have remained immovable and the contradiction between the principles has become a fundamental issue apparently without solution. In fact, the procedure of Beauchamp and Childress loses its meaning when the principles are not in contradiction. Despite this, Beauchamp and Childress have read the main feature of moral nature very well: the contradiction and its main challenge: to choose. However, they have not found a plausible solution that permits to end up the problem of principlism.

Principles of biomedical ethics are in constant tension. This means that the contradiction between them is part of the nature of Beauchamp and Childress' principlism; namely, it would not have any procedure if it would not have contradiction between principles. The value of The Principles of Biomedical Ethics is a parasitical value since it depends on the absence of contradiction. If such contradiction is insurmountable, those principles lose their objective value; that is, they loose their meening and their significance since they are not already effective to resolve any moral problem; namely, they are not longer applicable and it is necessary to appeal to casuistry.

I have to clarify here that overcoming the contradiction between principles is not the only solution for the problem of principlism. One solution is to rank them by applying plausible criteria. Other solutions are casuistry; that is, to eliminate principlism, i.e., not consider it anymore; and address moral problems with our common sense or individual inclinations; or redefine the principles and the procedure one uses when applying them in practice. This last approach gives principlism a higher objectivity in order to facilitate moral decisions making. This is my option because I think that we need principles to address moral conflicts. We have to seek objectivity and impartiality in moral deliberation. It is our duty. Making the best decision possible is always a moral obligation.

### III.3. The Contradiction Syndrome of Principlism

I will propose, without ignoring the value of Beauchamp and Childress principles as deliberative guidelines, some alternative principles to overcome what I call "the contradiction syndrome of principlism." Finding a reponse to the problem is not easy. Even my proposal is not a definitive reponse and it will certainly need application in different scenarios and more and better explanations to be considered plausible. However, I think that in the deliberative structure that I will offer, the applicability of principles does not depend of contradiction between them. In fact, deliberation does not need to be set in motion by contradiction. It is just necessary that one or more principles are violated; that is, the applicability of principles that I will propose does not depend on a formal fact but on a material or empirical one which occurs in the real world and that, thereby, is morally punishable. In this sense, unlike Beauchamp and Childress' principlism, the real grade of applicability of my

procedure does not depend on a logical criterium but on an ethical one.
On other hand, my proposal is also a response to critiques that I have mentioned above. My critique, even if recognizes, like Callahan, an ideological component in Beauchamp and Childress' principlism, which dangerously tends to relativism, does not oppose another ideology as solution. In this sense, I am not sustaining a tautological proposal.
I do not think that a unified moral theory can resolve all moral problems which, sometimes, are very specific and therefore require very specific and procedural solutions. Thus, my proposal also implies a procedure, so it is a principialist attempt to resolve, in a deliberative and dialogical way, moral problems that arise because of biomedical development. I do not aim to break principlism. I do not consider it a useless and inapplicable method, like Clouser and Gert thought.
Finally, the four European biolaw principles do not enlarge the epistemological scope of the procedure because those four principles are already tacitily implied in the Principles of Biomedical Ethics.
As from my earlier arguments, I propose the following principles and their respective procedimentation.

*Prevention*: Everyone has the right to be considered in the rational calculation that seeks to prevent possible risks and losses that could cause the execution of a particular action. This principle also protects the right that every human being has to act or allow to act on it, fully aware of possible risks, consequences and damage that such action could lead to.[191] This principle implies *Respect for Autonomy and Nonmaleficence*.

*Freedom*: The person has the right to decide his own life as the fruit of his identity, history, tradition and belief, namely, he has the right to be free to consider what it is good or right for himself, and to believe, practice and hold a truth in terms of his own cultural and religious identity. This principle implies *Respect for Autonomy* and *Beneficence*.

*Equality*: Every person has the duty to consider others on the same level as themselves. This means that others are also included on equal terms in the calculation that involves preventing the risks associated with any action. Moreover, this principle implies the obligation to protect individuals against any form of discrimination that violates or undermines their identity, dignity and status of end in themselves, and treats other as equal.[192] This principle implies *Justice*.

---

[191] This principle even could, for example, to include the principle of inviolability, which has been understood as follows: "What this offense embodies, I would suggest is a moral principle of considerable importance, the principle namely of the inviolability of the human body. According to this principle it is impermissible not only to intervene, penetrate, cut into the human body, but also to touch the skin or hair or even the clothes of a person without her consent. The consent required to avoid a violation of the principle can be assumed in certain circumstances, such as of a person who is unconscious as a result of an accident or of a young or unborn childe whose parents can be consulted". Gomez-Lobo, Alfonso, "The Ethical Evaluation of Human Cloning for Biomedical Research", in *Jahrbuch fur Wissenschaft und Ethik*, Berlin-New York, Walter de Gruvter, 2003, p. 14.

[192] Influential philosophers have stressed the procedural importance of equality between human beings. Singer has written, for example: "In the fifth century before the Christian era, the Chinese philosopher Mozi, appalled at the damage caused by war in his era, asked: 'What is the way of universal love and mutual benefit?' He answered his own question: 'It

*Good will*: Given the case, the person must be able to link his individual principles to binding minima. That is, he should be able to assume reasonably the primacy of universal values on its subjective maxima, avoiding moral relativism. Thus, he also can respect the duty not to seek to impose arbitrarily their ideas on others, because it restricts their scope because it respects pluralism on moral universalism. This principle implies *Respect for Autonomy*.

*Utilitarian evaluation*: When it is not possible to clearly determine the violation of the principles or, in the worst conceivable case, all of them are violated, the procedure provides this principle of exception to solve the problem, which it implies to make the decision that benefits the majority of individuals involved in the problem. This principle requires prudence and taking into account the responsibilities involved in the case.

The proposal includes, first, an individual level (Freedom and Good will) and a social level (Prevention, Equality and Utilitarian evaluation), and points out consequentialist principles (Freedom, Prevention and Utilitarian evaluation) and deontological ones (Equality and Good will).

---

is to regard other people's countries as one's own'. The ancient Greek iconoclast Diogenes, when asked what country he came from, is said to have replied: 'I am a citizen of the world'. In the late twentieth century John Lennon sang that it isn't hard to 'Imagine there's no countries…Imagine all the people/ Sharing all the world'. Until recentrly such thoughts have been the dreams of idealist, devoid of practical impact on the hard realities of a world of nation-states. But now we are beginning t olive in a global community." Singer, Peter, *One World. The Ethics of Globalization*, Second Edition, Yale University Press, 20042004, p. 196.

I have defined my principles avoiding the contradiction between them when they are applied in practice. Their definition is a complementary definition. These principles are cooperative and functional with each other, and though they stress specific rights and duties, they work as convergent guidelines that are not in contradiction in practice.

The application of these principles implies an arithmetic procedure. Faced with a specific case, we have to evaluate both possible courses of action, determining what principles are violated in each situation. We must then follow the option that violates the fewest principles. If in both courses of action the same number of principles is violated or it is very complicated to determine whether there is violation or not, we must use the principle of exception, which will ultimately determine what we should do.

This involves an inversely proportional relationship between the violation of principles and the morality of the act. In other words, when we violate a higher quantity of principles, the action is less plausible. Now, it is important to clarify that the arithmetic calculation is only a part of the procedure. The axiological evaluation and moral deliberation are present in the content of the principles.

This proposal is not a consumed model and it has yet to be empirically contrasted to prove its viability. However, my procedure has, at least, two features which could be promising: 1.The procedure eliminates the paralysis resulting from the inability to rank principles in complex cases—thus facilitating decision making in a way that is as objective as possible. 2. The procedure is

applicable not only on acts but also on legal rules, determining their fairness, effectiveness and plausibility.
But, does the procedure work? Let us check some real cases. With this, I only aim to show that my proposal is, at least, workable.

**CASE 1**

**Baby Theresa**

In 1992, the parents of an anencephalic baby named Baby Theresa wanted to donate her organs before her natural death. But the Florida Supreme Court did not allow it. She lived for ten days. When she died, her organs could no longer be transplanted.

**Procedure**

Question: Was the Florida Supreme Court's decision correct?

| Principles | Is there any violation? | Arguments |
|---|---|---|
| Prevention | YES/NO | On one hand, parents made the decision full informed about risks, damages and consequences. But, on other hand, we can clearly consider the act of killing Theresa as harmful. |
| Freedom | YES | On one hand, parents have made a decision from their own identity beliefs and wishes. On other, the act of killing |

| | | |
|---|---|---|
| | | Theresa is not strictly an act of beneficence because we do not have sufficient elements to affirm, from a mere quantitative point of view, that several lives have more value than only one. |
| Equality | YES | If Theresa had been a healthy girl no one would have thought of killing her to donate her organs. Her condition determined the parents' decision. |
| Good Will | YES | Parents are trying to impose their personal and individual wishes over a universal value like life in order to perform an apparently good purpose. |

Conclusion: The Florida Supreme Court's decision was correct.

**CASE 2**

**The Maltese Conjoined Twins**

Jodie and Mary were born as conjoined twins in August 2000. If they stayed together, both were going to die. If they were separated, Jodie was going to live and Mary was going to die. British physicians recommended surgery to separate them, but the parents refused to consent to separation because of their religious beliefs. However, the physicians turned to the courts for permission to perform the surgical separation without parental consent. Finally, the

Family Court of United Kingdom allowed the separation. Mary died. Jodie is still alive.

**Procedure**

Question: Was the Family Court´s decision correct?

| **Principles** | **Is there any violation?** | **Arguments** |
|---|---|---|
| Prevention | YES/NO | Parents know the consequences, risks and associated damages: one of the girls will die. But, we also can see a benefit: one of the conjoined twins has the real possibility of living. |
| Freedom | YES/NO | There are not sufficient elements to presume that both girls would agree with the final decision. Moreover, the Court prefered one life over another from a criterion of viability. |
| Equality | YES/NO | Do we have solid arguments to sustain the belief that Jodie´s life is more valuable than Mary´s? On other hand, we may sustain that, in this case, one life saved is better than both lost. |
| Good Will | NO | We can see that the parents had to prefer universal principles instead of individual |

| | | |
|---|---|---|
| | | ones because they did not agree with the surgical separation. |

Conclusion: In this more complex case we can use the principle of Utilitarian evaluation. From an intrinsic point of view, it is very difficult to demonstrate that one life has more value than another only because one of them is more viable. However, we can agree that given the imminent death of two persons and the possibility that one of them survives, the latter option is better. Therefore, the Court's decision was correct.

**CASE 3**

**Eluana Englaro´s Euthanasia**

Eluana Englaro was an Italian woman from Lecco, who entered a persistent vegetative state on January 18, 1992, following a car accident, and subsequently became the focus of a court battle between supporters and opponents of euthanasia. Shortly after Englaro had been fed with a feeding tube, her father requested to have her feeding tube removed and to allow her to die "naturally". The authorities initially refused his request, but this decision was later reversed after seventeen years.

**Procedure**

Question: Was the Italian authorities' decision correct?

| Principles | Is there any violation? | Arguments |
|---|---|---|
| Prevention | YES/NO | Family knows the consequences, but we do not have any way to communicate the decision to Eluana. However, she did not have possibilities to recover. |
| Freedom | NO | The family's decision is autonomus. |
| Equality | NO | There is equality because the authorities did not impose a supererogatory obligation on the family, the heavy burden of Eluana´s suffering. |
| Good Will | NO | There are no individual inclinations involved in the case. Letting Eluana die is an act of justice and dignity, for her and for her family. |

Conclusion: The final decision was correct.

Moreover, the procedure can be extended to problems related to Human Rights violation:

## CASE 4
## The Islamic Headscarf Ban in France

The French State adopted a legal rule which established a ban on students in public schools of using any object that was indicative of religious belief. A particular motivation for this rule was to prohibit the use of head coverings by Muslim women. Let us consider the case of a Muslim girl student who is faced with the ban at the same time she is pressured by her family who believes that a "decent girl" should cover her head in the public space. It is important to emphasize that this rule is still in place and is even being extended to all public space.

**Procedure**

Question: Can we affirm that the rule is fair?

| **Principles** | **Is there any violation?** | **Arguments** |
|---|---|---|
| Prevention | YES | The Muslim girl did not know about the rule before it came into effect. |
| Freedom | YES | The Muslim girl's freedom is clearly violated. |
| Equality | YES | The rule's motivation was discriminatory. It is not the same thing to hide a crucifix under the shirt as to take off a face covering in public because both acts have not the same meaning for those who perform them. |
| Good Will | YES | It does not seem legitimate, in this case, to force the Muslim girl to act contrary |

| | | |
|---|---|---|
| | | to her individual principles. |

Answer: The French rule is unfair.

After these examples, I have to clarify that I am looking for a procedure that demystifies not the contradiction between principles but the wrong belief that the discovery of this contradiction is a criterion to distinguish between the theoretical and general basis, and moral problems, always of a particular character. Every case must be considered in terms of the practical rationality intrinsic to this proposal, which avoids moral totalitarianism. Moreover, the general application protects society from moral liberalism (relativism). Thus, both levels are complementary in the pursuit of social understanding: deontological principles allow the justification of the procedure. Consequentialist principles are conducive to the exception in the application.

Therefore, my proposal challenges the reason beyond the traditional format of principlism because it requires impartial deliberation over issues that are particularly problematic for civil society. In summary, we should understand that if it is true that clear and well defined principles may signal the attainment of good ends, it is also true that, many times, the commitment to universal precepts at all costs which seem very plausible in theory - as currently happens with the classical structure of this procedure - can lead us to disastrous consequences.

My proposal recognizes individual rights (Freedom and Prevention), but also indicates obligations to others (Equality and Good will) and consideration of consequences to all involved in the case (Utilitarian evaluation). In this sense, I also understand principles as prima facie guidelines. I think that is not possible to rank the principles in practice from objective criteria. We can do it from casuistry, individual inclinations, even from caprices, but not from an impartial position. According to that reason I have thought about an arithmetical procedure, looking for more objectivity in decisions making.

Summarizing, my proposal implies a Decalogue; namely, it presents ten conditions of possibility:

1. *Violation*. The procedure does not consider contradiction as the motor of deliberation. The most important criterion to start the reasoning is the violation of principles and not their contradiction in practice.
2. *Dialogue*. The procedure it is not an ideology because it is not identified with only one current of thought. Therefore, my proposal permits and promotes dialogue between diverse philosophical doctrines, theoretical traditions and world conceptions, integrating all of them to deliberation in order to give the procedure more objectivity.
3. *Inclusion*. It is not a univocal procedure but an inclusive one. It considers diverse currents of thought.
4. *Extension*. It seeks to extend the epistemological and methodological scope of Beauchamp and Childress' principles, reinforcing the social meaning of new principles. However, that social meaning is not based in a communitarian ideology

but in a complementation between different branches of moral reasoning.

5. *Complementation.* It is a deliberative procedure that considers four principles as four guidelines that must be understood whitin a general framework of application. However, at the same time, my procedure considers the necessary exception in that application, proposing an explicit utilitarian criterion of exception in order to not paralyze deliberation when the case is particularly complex.
6. *Pluralism.* The procedure avoids, on one hand, moral universalism and ethical totalitarianism, and on other, moral relativism and ethical individualism.
7. *Consistency.* It is consistent with the nature of bioethics, because it is a procedure that implies pluralism and transdisciplinarity.
8. *Distinction.* It is not a tautological or repetitive procedure in relation to Beauchamp and Childress' principlism because it does not depend on the same criterion of deliberation.
9. *Argumentation.* It provides a legal argumentation's method in order to address cases related to human rights violation.
10. *Enlargement.* The procedure implies to enlarge the scope of the principles beyond science and medicine.

On the one hand, my procedure implies a consequentialist reason. In other words, the moral rightness criterion is based on the results of action. On the other hand, the deontological reason is applied to the necessary means for such consideration, namely, the duty to weigh the risks before acting and to consider the other as oneself. Thus, the imperative that I tacitly offer here does not refer to an ethics of intention, but an ethics of results; that is, an ethics not based on an *a priori* reason.

My proposal understands *a priori* reason as a means, by avoiding the mere utilitarian consideration of the consequences. In this way, I recognize that is not possible to find a theoretical and methodological equivalence between teleology and deontology into principlism and that we can only recognize a successive and not simultaneous presence of both deliberation moments. This I understand by complementariness between consequences and duties. Any other type of convergence would seem forced, capricious, made to measure, a sort of *haute couture* of principlism.

Moreover, and due to the impossibility of finding absolutely common ethical content in the moral strangers era, the most plausible way for a twenty-first century bioethics is to find a dialogical and argumentative procedure; namely, a procedure that does not transform individuals and that does not require them to alienate their nature and identity but, at first, push them to rationally anticipate the risks associated with the results of their action, considering the other as themselves. Thinking hypothetically, if we universalize the approach proposed by the imperative (to provide "reasonably" before acting), less damage would be possible for everyone and for all.

I should clarify here that this prevention does not refer to the globalized era typical prevention, which represents the impossibility of calculating any action effects. I do not understand the "rationally provide" maxim as an accurate and detailed account of consequences, but as a criterion for, first of all, being aware, and secondly, being responsible for any associated risks to the effects of our actions, without detriment of those risks can be invisible to any attempt of prediction. I propose a practical, dialogic and deliberative rationality, which is attentive to public space and its complex and changing phenomena. I do not propose a pure or axiomatic moral experience, but careful attitude to history and individual and social experience, which recognizes individual rights (Freedom and Prevention), but also indicates obligations to others (Equality and Good will).

Finally, for traditional ethics the moral rule should regulate human behavior. I propose a complementary procedure. In fact, I have not aspired only to prescribe but, most especially, I have tried to explain the current nature of existence. Bioethics should be characterized by seeking the convergence between different moments of moral reasoning which constitute our Western ethical heritage. Thereby, we must take into consideration one moment that cannot be ignored. Next to the Aristotelian moment of good life aspiration, and the Kantian moment of duties, bioethics should include a consequentialist moment which necessarily involves exemptions in the imperative application; namely, a moment of "practical wisdom" (*phronesis*), characterized by prudence. Therefore, bioethics must integrate teleology (end to get), deontology (duty to respect) and responsibility (consequences to consider) and recognize its basis in the Western philosophical-ethical tradition.

Only in this way, bioethics will be able to overcome its classic structure. Its goal should be to identify the essence of humanity beyond the modern subject conception. Bioethics is based on freedom and thereby opens the field of human thought beyond objective knowledge and the mere sense experience. Thus, principlism will be a plausible procedure from which to face the conflicts that underlie present existence and that claim to be urgently debated.

It is important to recognize the bioethical principles are in a permanent tension and are characterized by essential contradictions and deep dilemmas inherent in their theoretical and abstract nature. Therefore, as principles are related to welfare but also to the responsibility and social solidarity, they are too important and require more study and deepening. In this sense, I will try to integrate the principles in a framework that consider dialogue, freedom and the good will of human beings for resolving their mutual problems.

According to my own perspective, principlism requires changes and specifications because it represents a dynamic deliberative structure and thus it constitutes a challenge to the same bioethics. Therefore, principlism is not only a guideline for moral deliberation on problems related to the developing in the biomedicine and biotechnology. It represents the heart of bioethics, it is the core from which this discipline can project and designe a procedural structure to redefine our experiences of life and even give a new meaning for our existence. Bioethical principles reaffirm that behind scientific experimentation or medical treatment there are people who have rights and deserve to be respected in their status as persons. In this sense, bioethics recognizes the value of human beings beyond their differences in background, culture, race, religion, political beliefs, and philosophical ideas.

# REFERENCES


- Apel, Karl-Otto. "Diskursethik als Ethik Mitveranwortung für Kollektive Aktivitäten", in, *Rehabilitierung des Subjektiven*, ed. Hans-Joachim Waschkies, Bonn: Bouvier Verlag, 1993.

- Apel, Karl-Otto. "Fallibilismus. Konsenstheorie der Wahrheit und Letzbegründung", in *Philosophie und Begründung*, Frankfurt am Main: Suhrkamp, 1993.

- Aristotle, *Ethica Nicomachea (Nichomachean Ethics)*, in Mc Keon, Richard (Ed.) *The Basic Works of Aristotle*, New York, Random House, 1941.

- Aristotle, *Metaphysics*, New York, The Modern Library, 2001.

- Aristotle, *Organon*, New York, The Modern Library, 2001.

- Baker, Robert et al., *The Codification of Medical Morality*, vol. 1 and Baker, Robert (ed.), *The Codification of Medical*

*Morality*, vol. 2, Dordrecht/Boston, Kluwer Academic Publishers, 1995.

- Beauchamp, Tom L, "The Origins and Evolution of *The Belmont Report*", in Childress, James F; Meslin, Eric M; and Shapiro, Harold T. (Editors), *Belmont Revisited. Ethical Principles for Research with Human Subjects*, Georgetown University Press, 2005.

- Beauchamp, Tom L; and Childress, James F, *Principles of Biomedical Ethics,* Sixth Edition, Oxford University Press, New York, Oxford, 2009.

- Berlin Isaiah, *Four Essays on Liberty*, Oxford University Press, 1969.

- Brody, Baruch, *Taking Issue. Pluralism and Casuistry in Bioethics*, Georgetown University Press, 2003.

- Callahan, Daniel, "Individual Good and Common Good. A Communitarian Approach to Bioethics", in *Perspectives in Biology and Medicine*, 46, 4, Washington, DC, The John Hopkins University Press, 2003.

- Childress, James F; Meslin, Eric M; and Shapiro, Harold T. (Editors), *Belmont Revisited. Ethical Principles for Research with Human Subjects*, Georgetown University Press, 2005.

- Clouser, Danner and Gert, Bernard, "A Critique of Principlism", in *The Journal of Medicine and Philosophy*, Volume 15, Oxford University Press, 1990.

- Engelhardt, JR. Tristam H., *The Foundations of Bioethics*, Second Edition, Oxford University Press, 1996.

- Frankena, William, *Ethics*, Second Edition, New Jersey, Prentice Hall, 1973.

- Gomez-Lobo, Alfonso, "The Ethical Evaluation of Human Cloning for Biomedical Research", in *Jahrbuch fur Wissenschaft und Ethik*, Berlin-New York, Walter de Gruvter, 2003.

- Habermas, Jürgen, *Technology and Science as Ideology, Toward a Rational Society*, Beacon Press, Boston, 1970.

- Habermas, Jürgen, "Wahrheitstheorien, en H. Fahrenbach (comp.), *Wirklichkeit und Reflexion*, Pfullingen, Neske, 1973.

- Harvey, John Collins, "Andre Hellegers and Carroll House: Architect and Blueprint for the Kennedy Institute of Ethics," *Kennedy Institute of Ethics Journal*, Volume 14, Number 2, June 2004.

- Hume, David, *An Enquiry Concerning the Principles of Morals*, USA, Wilder Publications, 2008.

- Jahr, Fritz, (All in *Kosmos. Handweiser für Naturfreunde und Zentralblatt für das naturwissen-schaftliche Bildungs und Sammelwesen,* Stuttgart):

  - "Bio-Ethik, 1927.
  - "Der Tod und die Tiere," 1928.
  - "Tierschutz und Ethik," 1928.
  - "Soziale und sexuelle Ethik in der Tageszeitung," 1928.
  - "Wege zum sexuellen Ethos," 1928.
  - "Zwei ethische Probleme in ihrem Gegensatz und in ihrer Vereinigung im sozialen Leben," 1928.
  - "Egoism and Altruism,"1929.
  - "Gesinnungsdiktatur oder Gedankenfreiheit?" 1930.
  - "Unsere Zweifel an Gott," 1933.
  - "Drei Studiem zum 5. Gebot," 1934.
  - "Jenseitsglaube und Ethik im Christentum," 1934.
  - "Die sittlich-soziale Bedeutung des Sonntags," 1934.
  - "Zweifel an Jesus?" 1934.
  - "Ethische Betrachtungen zu innerkirchlichen Glaubenskämpfen," 1935.
  - "Glauben und Werkein ihrem Gegensatz und in ihrer Vereinigung," 1935.
  - "Drei Abschnitte des Lebens nach 2. Korinther," 1938.

- Jahr, Fritz, "Bio-Ethics. Reviewing the Ethical Relations of Humans towards Animals and Plants," in *Selected Essays in Bioethics 1927-1934 Fritz Jahr*, Zentrum fur Medizinische Ethik, Bochum, November 2010, Issue 186. Translation, Postcript and References by Hans-Martin Sass. "Bio-Ethik. Eine Umschau über die ethischen Beziehungen des Menschen zu Tier und Pflanze," in *Kosmos. Handweiser für Naturfreunde und Zentralblatt für das naturwissen-schaftliche Bildungs und Sammelwesen,* Stuttgart, 1927, 24(1): p. 2.

- Jahr, Fritz, "The Relationship of Animal Protection and Ethics, 1928," in *Selected Essays in Bioethics 1927-1934 Fritz Jahr*, Zentrum für Medizinische Ethik, Bochum, November 2010, Issue 186. Translation, Postcript and References by Hans-Martin Sass. ("Tierschuzt and Ethik," in *Aufsatze zur Bioethik 1927-1928 Fritz Jahr*. Nachwort und Nachweise von Hans-Martin Sass, Zentrum für Medizinische Ethik, Bochum, Dezember 2010, Issue 187.

- Jahr, Fritz, "Three Studies on the Fifth Commandment, 1934," in *Selected Essays in Bioethics 1927-1934 Fritz Jahr*, Zentrum für Medizinische Ethik, Bochum, November 2010, Issue 186. Translation, Postcript and References by Hans-Martin Sass. "Drei Studien zum 5. Gebot'" in *Kosmos. Handweiser für Naturfreunde und Zentralblatt für das naturwissen-schaftliche Bildungs und Sammelwesen,* Stuttgart, 1934, 10(1).

- Jonas, Hans, *Das Prinzip Veranwortung*: *Versuchi einer Ethic für die Tecnologische Zivilisation*, Francfort am Main, Insel Verlag, 1988.

- Jonas, Hans, *The Imperative of Responsibility. In Search of an Ethics for the Technological Age*, The University of Chicago Press, 1985.

- Jones, James H., *Bad Blood. The Tuskegee Syphilis Experiment*, New and Expanded Edition, New York, The Free Press, 1993.

- Jones, Roger C., Holden, Timothy, "A Guide to Assessing Decision Making Capacity'" in *Cleveland Clinic Journal of Medicine*, vol 71, 12, December 2004.

- Jonsen, Albert R.. *Bioethics beyond the Headlines*. New York, Rowman & Littlefield Publishers Inc., 2005.

- Jonsen, Albert R., *The Birth of Bioethics*, New York, Oxford University Press, 1998.

- Jonsen, Albert and Toulmin, Stephen, *The Abuse of Casuistry,* University of California Press, 1988.

- Kant, Immanuel, *Grounding for the Metaphysics of Morals*, 3rd ed. Hackett, Translate by James W. Ellington, 1993.

- Kant, Immanuel, *Fondements de la métaphysique des moeurs*, Paris, Librairie Delagrave, 1939; Translate by Victor Delbos.

- Macintyre, Alasdair, "Does applied ethics rest on a mistake?" in *The Monist*, 67, 1984.

- Mill, John Stuart, *Utilitarianism*, New York, The Liberal Arts Press, 1948.

- National Commission for the Protection of Human Subjects of Biomedical and Behavioral Research, *Belmont Report. Ethical Principles and Guidelines for the Protection of Human Subjects of Research*, US Government Printing Office, Reprint from the collection of the University of Michigan Library, 2009, Appendix Volume I, 78-0012.

- Ness, Bryan D., *Encyclopedia of Genetics*, Revised Edition, New Jersey, Salem Press Inc., 2004.

- *New York Times*, July 26, 1972, pp. 1, 8.

- Pellegrino, Edmund, "From Medical Ethics to a Moral Philosophy of the Profession," in Walter, Jennifer K., and

Klein, Eran P. (editors), *The Story of Bioethics*, Washington, DC, Georgetown University Press, 2003.

- Pence, Gregory E., *Classic Cases in Medical Ethics*, New York, Mc Graw Hill, 2004.

- Percival, Thomas, *Medical Ethics: or, a Code of Institutes and Precepts, Adapted to the Professional Conduct of Physicians and Surgeons*, London, S. Russell, 1803.

- Post, Stephen G., *Encyclopedia of Bioethics*, 3rd Edition, Macmillan Reference USA, 2004.

- Potter, Van Rensselaer "Bioethics: The Science of Survival," Persp. Biol. Med. 1970, 14(1).

- Raz, Joseph, *The Morality of Freedom*, Oxford, Clarendon Press, 198.

- Rehm, H.-J; Reed, G; Puhler, A; Stadler, P., *Biotechnology, Legal, Economical and Ethical Dimensions,* Second Completely Revised Edition, Germany, VCH Verlagsgesellschaft, 1995.

- Reich, Warren T., "The "Wider View": Andre Hellegers's Passionate, Integrating Intellect and the Creation of Bioethics,"

*Kennedy Institute of Ethics Journal*, Volume 9, Number 1, March 1999.

- Rendtorff, Jacob Dahl and Kemp, Peter, *Basic Ethical Principles in European Bioethics and Biolaw*, Vol. I, Report to the European Commission of the BIOMED-II Project, Guissona (Catalunya), Spain, Centre for Ethics and Law (Copenhagen) and Institut Borrja de Bioetica (Barcelona), 2000.

- Ross, W. David, *Foundations of Ethics*, London, Oxford at the Clarendon Press, 1951.

- Ross, W. David, *Kant's Ethical Theory*, Oxford, 1969. Also, Deleuze, Gilles, *La philosophie critique de Kant*, Paris, Presses Universitaires de France, 1963.

- Sass, Hans-Martin, "Aufsäzte zur Bioethik 1927-1938 Fritz Jahr," Nachwort und Nachweise von Hans-Martin Sass, *Zentrum für Medizinische Ethik*, Bochum, Dezember, 2010.

- Sass, Hans-Martin, "Fritz Jahr's 1927 Concept of Bioethics," *Kennedy Institute of Ethics Journal*, 2007, 17(4).

- Sass, Hans-Martin, "Poscriptum and References," in *Selected Essays in Bioethics 1927-1934 Fritz Jahr*, Zentrum für Medizinische Ethik, Bochum, November 2010, Issue 186.

- Sass, Hans-Martin, "Fritz Jahr's 1927 Concept of Bioethics," *Kennedy Institute of Ethics Journal* 17.4 (2007). Sass, Hans-Martin, "Fritz Jahr's 1927 Concept of Bioethics," *Kennedy Institute of Ethics Journal*, 2007, 17(4).

- Singer, Peter, *One World. The Ethics of Globalization*, Second Edition, Yale University Press, 2004.

- Teays, Wanda; Purdy, Laura, *Bioethics, Justice and Health Care*, USA, Wadsworth Thomson Learning, 2001.

- Toulmin, Stephen, S., The Tyranny of Principles. *Hastings Center Report* 11(6), 1981

- Valdes, Erick, *Bioethics for a Technological World*, Germany, VDM Verlag Dr. Müller, 2010.

- Valdes, Erick, *Critique of Globalized Reason. An Ethics for the Post-Enlightened Era*, Germany, VDM Verlag Dr. Müller, 2010.

- Van Renssealer Potter, *Bioethics. Bridge to the Future*, New Jersey, Prentice-Hall, 1971.

- Veatch, Robert, *The Basics of Bioethics*, Second Edition, New Jersey, Prentice Hall, 2003.

- Walter, Jennifer K. and Klein, Eran P. (Editors), *The Story of Bioethics. From Seminal Works to Contemporary Explorations*, Georgetown University Press, 2003.

- Weber, Max, *Le Savant et le Politique*, Paris, Éditions La Découverte, 2003.

**ON THE WEB**

- http://stemcells.nih.gov/info/basics/basics1.asp
- http://stemcells.nih.gov/info/basics/basics6.asp
- http://www.genome.gov/Glossary/index.cfm?id=173.
  http://www.genome.gov/Glossary/index.cfm?id=199.
- http://willson.cm.utexas.edu/Research/Sub_Files/Biochip/index.php, University of Texas.

Made in the USA
Columbia, SC
29 August 2020

18506061R00109